Additional Praise for
The Open Innovation Revolution

"*The Open Innovation Revolution* provides an excellent and extremely practical overview of the strategies and skills required to succeed at open innovation, from one of the leading global experts on the topic."

Roland Harwood,
Open Innovation Director, NESTA; Cofounder, 100%Open

"*The Open Innovation Revolution* is a good reference for anyone leveraging an open innovation model. Stefan helps us understand what open innovation looks like and what types of people and skills are necessary to operate in a networked open innovation culture."

Cheryl Perkins,
Founder and President, Innovationedge

"The first essential resource for practitioners interested in reinventing R&D for a new era."

Chris Trimble,
Coauthor, *The Other Side of Innovation*; Adjunct Associate Professor of Business Administration, Tuck School of Business, Dartmouth

"Every corporate intrapreneur needs to know that the challenges he or she faces are not as unique and daunting as they may at first seem. "Innovate or die" is the watchword today for Western firms facing the tsunami of global competition. This book is the 21st century version of *The Art of War*, written thoughtfully, with handy and convenient examples. Its intrapreneur readers will become a community with common purpose which spans industries and borders."

Ken Morse,
Founding Managing Director, MIT Entrepreneurship Center; Chair, Innovation, Entrepreneurship, and Competitiveness, Delft University of Technology

The Open Innovation Revolution

ESSENTIALS, ROADBLOCKS, AND LEADERSHIP SKILLS

Stefan Lindegaard

Foreword by
Guy Kawasaki

WILEY

John Wiley & Sons, Inc.

Published by John Wiley & Sons, Inc., Hoboken, New Jersey.
Published simultaneously in Canada.

For general information on our other products and services or for technical
support, please contact our Customer Care Department within the United States at
(800) 762-2974, outside the United States at (317) 572-3993 or fax (317) 572-4002.

Wiley also publishes its books in a variety of electronic formats. Some content that
appears in print may not be available in electronic books. For more information
about Wiley products, visit our web site at www.wiley.com.

Library of Congress Cataloging-in-Publication Data:

Lindegaard, Stefan.
    The open innovation revolution : essentials, roadblocks, and leadership
skills / Stefan Lindegaard ; foreword by Guy Kawasaki.
        p.   cm.
    Includes bibliographical references and index.
    ISBN 978-0-470-60439-7 (cloth)
        1. Technological innovations. 2. Entrepreneurship.   3. Leadership.
    I. Title.
    HD45.L527   2010
    658.4'063—dc22

                                                              2009054063

Printed in the United States of America

10   9   8   7   6   5   4   3   2   1

Contents

Foreword

I 've often heard entrepreneurs at start-up companies express envy for intrapreneurs working in large companies. According to the struggling, boot-strapping entrepreneurs, these internal innovators are living large. They supposedly have access to everything entrepreneurs lack: ample capital, comfy infrastructure, and an established umbrella brand. Who couldn't succeed in such an environment?

This viewpoint overlooks two harsh facts of life that many intrapreneurs cope with daily. First, they are not just handed the key to the company cashbox; they often have to fight tooth and nail for the financial and human resources needed to get their projects off the ground and keep them moving forward. Second, they are up against an army of people who are fiercely dedicated to maintaining the corporate status quo. Faced with inbred, ingrained, and, let's be blunt, sometimes inept management, intrapreneurs struggle to unleash entrepreneurial thinking at established companies while compensating for these unique challenges.

In short, life is not exactly a bed of roses for most intrapreneurs. They face down challenges that would cause less passionate, less driven, and less talented people to quickly throw up their hands in defeat. This is why I love intrapreneurs. They foster the pluck and creativity companies need to stay ahead of the pack. They shake things up. They take on sacred cows. They build new futures for their companies. It's exciting stuff!

It's clear from this book that Stefan Lindegaard loves intrapreneurs, too. He clearly understands them and the world they live in at work. He has provided a thoughtful, practical guide for how corporate innovation leaders and intrapreneurs can take on the new challenge that all corporate innovators face: how to operate in a world of open innovation, where new skills are needed to foster the external relationships that will be essential to staying ahead of the competition when knowledge flows freely around a world that is open for business 24/7.

As this book makes clear, Stefan gets that intrapreneurial success is all about people. Sure, you need to have effective innovation processes in place; there's no denying that. But, as Stefan makes clear, without the right people to drive those processes, your odds of success shrink dramatically. And as open innovation becomes the norm, developing the right people skills, including networking, communicating with stakeholders, building your personal brand, and the ability to sell ideas,is essential for every innovation leader and intrapreneur. Stefan provides the rationale for developing these skills and then tells you how to go about honing these capabilities so that you're able to perform at your best in the brave new world of open innovation.

I would like particularly to draw your attention to Part II of this book in which Stefan lays out the roadblocks that corporate innovation leaders and intrapreneurs face as they go up against the corporate antibodies and the senior executives who don't always understand innovation or provide the necessary support. As Sun Tzu advised in *The Art of War*, it is important to "know your enemy," and while it may be uncomfortable to think in those terms, the reality is that anyone who is trying to bring a corporation kicking and screaming into the future will generate a lot of heat from those with a vested interest in keeping things the way they are. Stefan provides a wealth of advice on how to fight the forces of the status quo, including one I've always loved, which is stay under the radar. Staying invisible for as long as possible will help you avoid a lot of the flak that starts flying as soon as any new idea surfaces.

That is just one small piece of the helpful information you'll find in these covers. I am confident you will be better armed to fight the intrapreneurial battle after reading this book. Enjoy!

GUY KAWASAKI
Founder, Alltop.com
Author, *Reality Check*

Introduction

T he world of innovation, where I've worked for the past 11 years of my life, is in the midst of a dramatic shift. Companies around the world are opening up their innovation process to include external partners of all types, including suppliers, customers, academics, competitors, and entrepreneurs with great ideas or unique capabilities. It may be too soon to call it a revolution—although some people perceive it as such—but a paradigm shift is definitely occurring right now.

This book provides you with ideas about how your company can be part of this open innovation revolution or paradigm shift. This requires a strong foundation for innovation in your company and a new mindset and new skills for you as an individual, all of which are described in these pages. My goal is to help you determine if moving toward open innovation is the right choice for your organization and then to show you how to prepare yourself and your people to make the leap into this challenging, yet highly exciting new environment.

As you read this book, you will find that I use many examples of my personal interactions with innovation leaders. Many are about innovation in general—and not just open innovation—but I believe these insights are valuable as you prepare your company and yourself for the open innovation revolution. So who am I, and why am I so passionate about the topic of innovation leadership?

My short biography says that I am a speaker, network facilitator, and strategic advisor who helps companies on topics such as open innovation, intrapreneurship, and how to identify and develop the people who drive innovation. I am the initiator and facilitator of physical network groups in Europe and the United States for people working at the intersection of leadership and innovation. I also run the LinkedIn community 15inno, which has more than 800 innovation leaders and intrapreneurs from companies around the globe as well as many consultants, academics, startups, and other people interested in innovation.

I have had the privilege of working with innovation leaders and intrapreneurs for many years now. They are great people with tough jobs. In a world where change is everywhere and faster than ever, where opportunities are limitless, their top management trusts them to make things happen.

The key objective of innovation leaders and intrapreneurs is to identify and develop profitable growth opportunities. Often, they are also in charge of transforming the corporate culture to become more innovative and entrepreneurial. Can job objectives get more exciting than this? If you ask an innovation leader, you will get a passionate answer: "This is just great, and I love my job."

Innovation leaders and intrapreneurs are passionate and see challenges as opportunities to prove that they excel within their chosen areas. They overcome obstacles every day and occasionally they move mountains. They are great assets to companies if used correctly. Management has begun to realize this during a long period in which they focused on and invested heavily in innovation and entrepreneurship.

I have worked with these great people, I have seen what they are capable of, and I want to help them become even better at making a difference and at identifying and developing new growth opportunities. That is my reason for writing this book in which we will look at:

- Open innovation, a model that more and more companies are adopting in response to a world increasingly characterized by global business entities and open sharing of information.
- The people who make innovation happen—including innovation leaders and intrapreneurs—and the essential elements that must be put in place for these people to thrive.
- People-related roadblocks that can impede innovation and some ways these can be overcome.
- The personal leadership skills you will need to develop as an innovation leader or intrapreneur.

In a bonus chapter (Chapter 17), I'll describe how you can use corporate business plan competitions to identify intrapreneurs within your organization and also build skills needed to tackle open innovation. Along the way, you'll also hear directly from innovation leaders through a series of interviews.

Each chapter ends with a list of key takeaways; these are gathered in one place in the book's final chapter so you have one easy place to go whenever you want to quickly review what you've learned.

Although challenging, open innovation carries with it a world of possibilities for new business ideas and business growth. I hope you'll enjoy the ride!

PART

I

THE ESSENTIALS

In this part of the book, I look into the current state of affairs with open innovation and the essential people-related elements that must be in place for open innovation—or indeed innovation of any type—to flourish. Most critically, the importance of identifying the right people is something that simply cannot be stressed enough. Yet all too often, I find that companies are far more focused on process than on the people part of open innovation. Don't get me wrong. Getting the right innovation processes in place is important, particularly as you move toward the more complicated world of open innovation, But nothing happens unless you have the right people with the right mindset and skills in the right place at the right time. This portion of the book is designed to help you do just that.

CHAPTER 1

Why Open Innovation Matters

In my travels, I have found that open innovation is not yet fully understood by many companies. Some people argue that the buzz about open innovation that has cropped up in the past few years is hype. I disagree; I believe open innovation is just getting started, and the main reason for this is that open innovation rides on two global megatrends:

1. Innovation has become a global 24/7 operation. Many companies have set up R&D and innovation labs outside their corporate headquarters, stretching the possibilities for how innovation is done, and making it easier for companies to take the logical next step of opening up their innovation processes to external partners.
2. The other megatrend is the transparency of knowledge. We all know that what really matters in our companies is knowledge. But where does this knowledge reside? For the most part, it is inside our heads, although the emergence of knowledge management as a discipline over the past two decades has created methods for companies to better tap into the knowledge embedded in their people and their experiences. Still, distributing knowledge within organizations remains challenging, and becomes even harder when you have to extend that knowledge outside the corporate boundaries as well. But we now live in a global world where knowledge is becoming more accessible and transparent. This makes

3

it easier to innovate across barriers. Web 2.0 tools such as wikis are being adapted by companies that also have begun to see professional value in social networking platforms such as LinkedIn and Facebook. Finding people who have the knowledge you need has never been easier, thanks to such networking tools.

One small sign of the increasing interest in open innovation is the fact that the number of LinkedIn profiles with the term *open innovation* is growing fast. This could be a sign of hype, but I have checked many of these profiles when I invite new members to join our 15inno community on LinkedIn and have found that there is real substance behind the profiles. If you dig further into the profiles, you understand that many companies have started interesting open innovation initiatives. You can also see this at innovation conferences. In these difficult economic times, open innovation is the only topic that seems to be able to draw an audience.

Challenges Abound

There is a lot of talk about how to define open innovation. I try not to get into definitions and semantics as I believe it is important for companies to define this broad term to match their own situation. However, I will add that, to me, open innovation is very much about bridging internal and external resources to make innovation happen.

Actually, one of the chief challenges posed by open innovation was neatly summed up in this comment by a participant in one of my Danish network groups for innovation leaders: "Embracing the outside requires that you really know the inside." There is no reason to go outside corporate boundaries if the company does not know what is happening within the company. Internal and external resources need to work hand in hand to make open innovation happen.

I also fully acknowledge that open innovation should be viewed as a two-way process in which companies have an inbound process in which they bring in ideas, technologies, or other resources needed to develop their own business and an outbound-process in which they out-license or sell their own ideas, technologies, and other resources. This should take place during all stages of the innovation process.

Nevertheless, I believe companies have plenty of challenges just making the inbound process work and they need to focus on this. As they get the proper mindset and processes in place, then they can start looking into the outbound processes in which they out-license or sell technologies, ideas, or intellectual property not being used internally. But focus is important in order to get it right in the first place. Thus, in this book, open innovation is almost entirely about the inbound process.

It is my firm belief that open innovation should be a hot topic at every company that is serious about innovation. Why? Because the idea of combining internal and external resources to increase innovation productivity and prowess is just too good a value proposition to miss out on. Take consumer-goods giant Procter & Gamble (P&G) as an example. Since 2001 P&G's innovation success rate has more than doubled, while the cost of innovation has fallen. Joachim von Heimburg, who has 30 years of experience with P&G, told my Danish network groups that he believes many companies can get similar gains if they make open innovation a part of their overall innovation strategy.

But here is the problem. Almost all companies have a marketing strategy or a sales strategy, but only very few companies have an innovation strategy. When companies have an innovation strategy, it is also important that they do not just put open innovation on top of this. According to von Heimburg, companies can only increase their innovation productivity if open innovation becomes an integrated part of such a strategy.

I believe that, as of now, only about 10 percent of all companies are adept enough at open innovation to get significant benefits. Let's call them the champs. Another 30 percent have seen the light and are scrambling to make open innovation work and provide results that are worth the effort. I call them contenders. The other 60 percent are pretenders—companies that don't really know what open innovation is and why or how it could be relevant for their companies. Some might figure out how to follow the leaders one day, but today they're going through the motions.

Obviously, P&G is an uncontested champ, as I explain in the sidebar at the end of this chapter. Its management no longer views open innovation as something new, unique, and different. After nine years, it is just the way the company innovates. Not many other have reached this level of confidence.

Intuit and General Mills seem to be champs in the making. The reason I like Intuit is its Entrepreneur Day initiative, which they held for the first time in late 2009 for 40 selected start-up companies. Although I have not yet heard of specific outcomes on this initiative, I find it to be a great display of setting clear goals, establishing a filter process, and showing strong commitment toward creating new partnerships. All are important aspects for open innovation.

At a first glance, the portal for General Mills Worldwide Innovation Network (G-WIN) in which General Mills seeks new technologies applicable for their current lines of business looks just like the many other open-innovation portals that are popping up right now. But based on an interview with Jeff Bellairs, who directs General Mills' Worldwide Innovation Network, I picked up on some sharp thinking behind the scenes.

What I like in particular is that General Mills is making the linkage between outside and inside resources as smooth as possible. One of their tools for this is an "external speed team," a cross-functional group that meets biweekly to discuss projects, share insights, and make sure its external partners are talking with the right people. In addition, General Mills recently launched an innovation entrepreneur program. These individuals have a number of responsibilities, including ensuring that outside ideas make their way into the company's innovation pipeline.

The efforts by General Mills are highly relevant as they can help General Mills reach one of the key objectives which is to become the preferred partner of choice. Such a position brings a first-hand look at new technologies and ideas, and this advantage is very important in the long run. This requires effective processes for linking internal and external resources. General Mills understands this. (See the complete interview with Jeff Bellairs at the end of Chapter 3.)

Campbell Soup jumped on open innovation through its Ideas for Innovation portal in 2009. Unfortunately, this is more like a gimmick than a serious attempt to engage customers and business partners, so I'm putting Campbell in the pretender category. While I'm singling Campbell out, the truth is that many other companies are just as clueless. Here are my specific problems with Campbell:

- Its intentions are too vague and unfocused. Campbell declares that it wants "ideas for new products, packaging, marketing, and production technologies that will help us meet the needs of our consumers and customers better, faster, and more completely." Gee, that could be almost anything, couldn't it?

- The company should be turning us on, not away. Campbell says it will take three to six months to respond to a suggestion, and if it turns down your idea, you won't receive any explanation. Why not try to make it more inviting?
- The whole thing reads like an ego trip. The Campbell web site talks only about why open innovation is good for Campbell. If Campbell wants help, it should at least mention how collaboration can help its would-be partners.

Although Campbell is pleased by receiving nearly 5,000 submissions, they acknowledge that their efforts in this space are not perfect and they are working on future enhancements of the site to move from the pretender and contender ranks to the championship level; here are issues that Campbell (or anyone else) needs to deal with early in the process.

First of all, you need to ask the why question. Many people jump into open innovation without asking why it is relevant to their particular situation. Open innovation works only if it aligns with the overall corporate strategy. Many companies mess up here. They simply do not have an innovation strategy.

The next step is defining what open innovation is. Innovation, and even more so open innovation, can be defined in many different ways. Companies need to know what they're after, as Procter & Gamble and General Mills do.

Before moving on to implementation, you must remember your people. A paradigm shift requires that employees change their mindset and obtain new skills. The keys to open innovation are the abilities to view innovation in more holistic terms and to become better networkers.

Open innovation is by no means easy. But as I said at the start, the value proposition is just too good to miss out on.

Admittedly, it is difficult to find hard evidence that the benefits of open innovation outweigh its costs. Not much research has yet been done. A recent report from the Belgian management school, Vlerick Leuven Gent, where researchers Dr. Dries Faems and Dr. Matthias de Visser (Universiteit Twente) and Prof. Bart Van Looy and Dr. Petra Andries (Katholieke Universiteit Leuven) studied joint ventures and open innovation and came to the conclusion that, in the short term, the financial costs of innovative joint-venture projects are greater than the financial benefits.

In their research, they studied the collaborative activities and the financial performance of 305 Belgian industrial companies. They found that collaborating with several partners does produce greater innovative strength, but it also increases the proportion of employee expenses in the added value, which in turn has a negative effect on financial performance. In the short term, it appears that this cost-raising effect is even greater than the indirect value-creating effect of the joint venture.

Do these findings signify the end of open innovation? The researchers don't think so. The innovative and financial-surplus value of joint-venture initiatives does become evident over the long term. In evaluating open innovation models, people in the public as well as the private sector often want to see quick results. Indeed, in the short term the costs are particularly visible, while the benefits take longer to manifest. A bit of patience and staying power are apparently essential.

P&G: How Open Innovation Is Done

The world's largest consumer-packaged goods giant, Procter & Gamble, operated one of the most widely admired and successful research and development operations in corporate history. But its closed innovation model suffered from a not-invented-here syndrome and was not up to the task of driving the corporate growth needed to sustain an enterprise of P&G's size. So in 2000, under the leadership of the newly appointed CEO A. G. Lafley, P&G began looking for a better global innovation model. Lafley soon expressed the radical idea that half of the company's innovation output should include a key external contribution.

What set P&G off toward an open innovation model was the discovery that there were 200 researchers and scientists outside P&G who were just as good or even better for each of P&G's own 7,500 researchers and scientists. That adds up to perhaps 1.5 million people whose talent the company could potentially tap into. What would an arrogant company do with such a learning experience? You are right. They would say it did not matter. They would argue that since they are not on their payroll there is no reason to care about them. P&G chose not to be arrogant and instead explored ways of working with these 1.5 million great minds. Eight years later, P&G had 9,000 scientists within the company and estimated they had access to two million externally. Many of these outside scientist and engineers work at the small or mid-sized entrepreneurial firms that are increasingly the locus for important innovation.

P&G adopted an innovation model they called Connect+Develop. It's a two-way street, accessing externally developed intellectual property in its own markets while allowing its internally developed assets and know-how to be used by others. It collaborates with individuals and companies, laboratories, research institutes, financial institutions, suppliers, academia, and R&D networks. A team of more than 50 people searches for open innovation opportunities in engineering, technology, trademarks, packaging, and more.

Today, a web site dedicated to Connect+Develop (www .pgconnectdevelop.com) is the cornerstone in bridging internal and external resources. A visit to the web site highlights that open innovation to P&G is about much more than just technology transfer. It encompasses everything from trademarks to packaging, marketing models to engineering, and business services to design. The site is not just for soliciting ideas; the team is actively seeking those who have already patented their ideas and need P&G's help in bringing them to market. This approach has already resulted in more than 1,000 active agreements between P&G and external partners.

I like the example of Pringle chips with text or images. It started with a great idea inside P&G, but the technology to make this happen was found in a small bakery in Bologna, Italy, run by a professor who had invented a technology that uses ink-jet techniques to print pictures on pastries. P&G got their hands on the technology making it possible to launch the new Pringles Prints chips in less than a year—and at a fraction of the cost of doing it in house.

As reported in a 2006 *Harvard Business Review* article authored by two P&G executives, the company's innovation success rate has more than doubled while the cost of innovation has fallen.[1] The company is close to reaching Lafley's goal of having half of their innovation coming from external sources.

Interestingly, employees were not given any additional incentives to change their not-invented-here mindset. Instead, persistence by R&D management in general and by Lafley in particular did the trick. Lafley used every occasion to ask for updates on the progress toward

(continued)

his stated goal. This CEO did not give up, and bit by bit the new mindset took root in the company. Many of these employees are very appreciative because P&G has embraced a proudly found-elsewhere culture that gives them many more opportunities to make innovation happen.

By the way, if you want to get an idea of how oriented a company is toward open innovation, you should take a look at their corporate web site. Try doing this with Procter & Gamble at www.pg.com. Scroll the page, and you will find a link to the Connect+Develop web site. Yes, this seems obvious, but nevertheless very few companies have made this small effort to make it easy for external partners to approach them. This is just one sign that open innovation is not a new and unique gimmick at Procter & Gamble. This is just the way they innovate.

Key Chapter Takeaways

- The 24/7 global economy and the increasing transparency of knowledge are driving the movement toward open innovation.
- Internal and external resources need to work hand-in-hand to make open innovation happen.
- Open innovation should be a hot topic in every company because the idea of combining internal and external resources to increase innovation productivity and prowess is just too good a value proposition to ignore.
- There are champs, contenders, and pretenders in the open-innovation world, with as many as 60 percent of companies falling in the pretender category.
- To move out of the pretender category and into the contender category, you must do these things:
  - Ask why your company should be involved in open innovation. Open innovation works only if your reasons align with the overall corporate strategy.
  - Define what open innovation is.
  - Remember your people. A paradigm shift like this requires that employees change their mindset and obtain new skills.

2

What Open Innovation Looks Like

The form open innovation takes can vary dramatically from company to company. In fact, there isn't a generally accepted definition of open innovation; ask 10 people what it is, and you'll get 10 different answers.

As mentioned earlier, we should not get too much into semantics and definitions as companies need to define this concept according to their own situations. However, it may be helpful to look at what constitutes *closed* innovation as a way to make the task of defining its opposite—open innovation—easier. Everyone seems to agree that closed innovation involves keeping discoveries highly secret while maintaining complete control over all aspects of the innovation process. In closed innovation, you do not attempt to assimilate input from outside sources into the innovation process, and you avoid having to share intellectual property or profits with any outside source.

Also, in a closed innovation environment, activities are often segregated within an R&D department, where the best and the brightest are expected to make sure the company gets to market early with new ideas to gain the first-mover advantage.

In direct contrast, open innovation is about bridging internal and external resources throughout the entire innovation process to make innovation happen. The first steps of open innovation in many companies often focus only on soliciting ideas from outside, but, in fact, real open innovation goes deeper than just involving others in the idea generation phases. The contribution from outside your company must be significant. It is also more than just a partnership in which you pay for specific services. Everyone involved in an open innovation process focuses on problems, needs, and issues and works them out *together*. Furthermore, you can argue that closed innovation primarily focuses on the core products and services, whereas you are more likely to use open innovation to work with a broader range of the Ten Types of Innovation (see Appendix), including business models, channels, and processes.

Variations exist on the open innovation process, and I believe the real differentiator among them is the level of involvement from external partners, customers, or suppliers. Many companies rely on their users for feedback and input about how to further develop their products or services, or even to think up new offerings. This is often referred to as user-driven innovation. Companies should look into this as a way of understanding and reacting to the needs of its users and customers. However, you cannot rely solely on user-driven innovation, because this approach often ends up just being a feedback tool, used primarily in the early idea-generating phases and later as you set up a feedback loop. Even though ideas may be sourced from outside, the idea is turned into a business almost entirely through internal innovation capabilities. There is no external involvement in the later phases.

User-driven is highly related to open innovation, but it has to go further to become open innovation. This happens when you not only get ideas from external sources but also let external sources become key players in the process of turning ideas into a business. Denmark has its share of world-leading companies on user-driven innovation. Lego, the toy company, is a great example of this through their Adult Fan of Lego groups and many other initiatives. The similarities and differences of user-driven innovation and open innovation are nicely illustrated by looking at a couple of Lego projects:

- **User-driven innovation—LEGO Mindstorms:** This line of Lego sets combines programmable bricks with electric motors, sensors, Lego bricks, and Lego Technic pieces (such as gears, axles, and beams). It has been a huge hit, and early on adult fans of Lego (AFOLs) were invited to help develop new designs and uses for Mindstorms. Nevertheless, Lego still controls the value chain almost 100 percent. This is changing as some AFOLs have started their own companies and have begun working with Lego in a more formal manner. I think this is a good example of user-driven innovation that has the potential to become open innovation.

- **Open innovation—LEGO Architectures:** In July 2008, Lego announced a partnership with Brickstructures, Inc., a privately held company established to promote the use of LEGO Bricks in relation to architecture. The idea is to offer a line of famous landmarks from around the world celebrating influential architects and movements that have shaped cities and cultures. With models developed in collaboration with architects, LEGO Architecture will work to inspire future architects, engineers, and designers around the world with the LEGO brick as a medium. Brickstructures bring the knowledge of architecture to the table. This is key input to the joint venture. I think this is closer to open innovation than the Lego Mindstorm example.

Another Danish company that effectively uses user-driven innovation is Coloplast, which develops products and services that make life easier for people with very personal and private medical conditions. Their business includes ostomy care, urology and continence care, and wound and skin care. They are considered by many as a global pioneer of user-driven innovation due to their work with doctors, nurses, and users of their products.

Coloplast has set up communities for their users to share experiences and ideas. You can check out one of their communities on www.stoma-innovation.com. Coloplast claims they have halved their development time over the last couple of years partly due to the external input, and they also mention that they are now using many more external partners than previously.

It sounds good, but nevertheless, I think Coloplast is a nice example of company that is still stuck in the user-driven mindset. The main idea of user-driven innovation is to get input from the users—and perhaps even the ecosystem—of your products or services.

Open innovation is about integrating external partners in the entire innovation process. This should happen not just in the idea or technology-development phase but also in all other phases toward market acceptance. User-driven innovation is great because it directs your innovation efforts toward market needs. Open innovation takes you to the next step by providing more opportunities through external partners as you address those market needs.

Which red flags did I pick up on Coloplast? First, take at look at their corporate web site. I cannot find any guidelines on how to approach Coloplast with ideas or other contributions. Compare this to P&G where, as I mentioned earlier, you can find a very visible link to their Connect+Develop initiative.

Another red flag is the stoma community itself. It really gives you the feeling that it is about how Coloplast can tap into users rather than how they can work together and build relationships with external partners. This is what user-driven innovation is about. However, it should not be confused with open innovation.

Furthermore, if you search for *innovation* on Coloplast' corporate web site, nothing shows up besides a link to their international stoma community. This is actually a bit scary for a company that perceives itself as being quite innovative. It makes me—and perhaps many others—wonder how serious they really are about innovation . . .

If I had the ear of someone at Colopast, I would caution them, and other companies as well, not to be confused by the two types of innovation. This confusion can be misleading and can damage the possibilities of a company becoming the preferred partner of choice, which is a key objective on the open innovation game.

A blog I posted entitled "Why User-driven Innovation Shouldn't Be Confused with Open Innovation" generated a flurry of feedback that illustrated just how confusing differentiating between user-driven innovation and open innovation can be. Ellen Di Resta, of the innovation consulting firm Synaptics Group, suggested that we should "view user-innovation and open innovation as approaches. Thinking of it that way, then it's the application of an approach that needs to be tailored to each specific context." She also mentioned that the terms can be ambiguous, and asked whether this might not be the point as it keeps us from being boxed too narrowly into a corner when we may need our tools to be flexible enough to handle a broad range of challenges.

Jeff Murphy, a corporate guy from Johnson & Johnson, made this statement: "I prefer to view open innovation as a broad enough term that also includes what you have referred to as 'user-driven innovation.'" He also mentioned that ". . . rather than getting tangled in semantics, I see it as more productive for an organization to select and use the right types of open innovation—those that are best aligned with their organization's specific needs, objectives, and business/technical complexity."

As stated earlier, user-driven innovation and open innovation mean different things to many people. The two types of innovation are related but not the same, and we currently find ourselves in a situation in which open innovation and user-driven innovation already have so many different meanings and definitions that it becomes useless for academics and consultants to drive *one* definition for these terms. This takes us back to the importance of having companies develop their own definition of open innovation.

As a last note on this, I think user-driven and open innovation can be a powerful combination, and I believe we will see great instances of this occurring as both user-driven and open innovation continue to evolve.

Benefits, Challenges, and Stumbling Blocks

The early stages of open innovation already take place in a lot of companies. In fact, almost any company can point to examples of innovation activities that differ from the closed model in ways that would be defined as open innovation. But the level ranges from a paltry few percent of the overall innovation effort for very inwardly focused companies to the amazing level of nearly 50 percent that P&G has reached. No matter where your company is now on this spectrum, the key thing to understand is that open innovation is the future, so it's important to start making some form of open innovation part of your overall strategy. The generally accepted main benefits of open innovation are to:

- Speed the development of new products and services and thus increase revenues and market share.
- Shorten time to market for new products and services and accelerate profits.
- Reduce direct spending on R&D.
- Improve the success rate of new products and services.[1]

Of course, open innovation offers challenges, as well, especially for aspiring and current managers and leaders who are accustomed to working in a closed innovation environment. These three fundamental questions must be answered before embarking on a journey toward open innovation:

1. **What will open innovation do to your business model?** In an open innovation world, you may end up working with any-one—even competitors. How will this impact your business model and alter your competitive landscape?
2. **How will your organizational chart change to accommodate open innovation?** What kind of collaborations do you want to engage in? What common vision and mission will you share with partners? Systems, processes, values, and culture across the company will need to be transformed. People who have spent their careers being internally focused now must focus externally as well.
3. **What does this mean to my role as manager or leader?** Many organizations have not mastered the ability to innovate across different business areas internally, let alone doing so with outside partners. As a result, many managers and leaders do not understand open innovation at a basic level. They need to understand the impact of this movement—its opportunities and threats—and learn to adopt a leadership style that optimizes trust, motivation, and performance.

I will get more into the roadblocks for open innovation—and innovation in general—in Part II.

Innovation Marketplaces: A Major Resource for Open Innovation

As open innovation becomes more widespread, the need increases for innovation marketplaces that can serve as intermediaries to which companies can quickly connect. Some of these intermediaries will serve niche markets, whereas others will be more general. Some will be set up by companies to meet their specific needs, and others will be set up by third parties that want to position themselves as an interface between companies seeking solutions and the smart people—or companies—with solutions.

InnoCentive is a third-party innovation marketplace that operates with a prize-based open innovation model. InnoCentive connects companies, academic institutions, the public sector, and nonprofit organizations with a global network of more than 160,000 experts and problem solvers in 175 countries around the world. InnoCentive was originally developed by pharmaceutical giant Eli Lilly as an in-house innovation incubator. An independent organization since 2005, InnoCentive initially saw success within the pharmaceutical marketplace, but it is now active in many other industries, including consumer packaged goods, where companies such as P&G have had success using InnoCentive.

InnoCentive's process works like this: An organization (a seeker) provides a challenge to solvers all over the world who can win cash prizes for solving the problem. More than a third of the solvers have doctorates. Problems have been presented in engineering, computer science, math, chemistry, life sciences, physical sciences, and business. InnoCentive gets a posting fee and a finder's fee if the problem is solved.

Of course, InnoCentive has competition. Here are few other open innovation marketplaces:

- NineSigma provides an extensive global network of scientists, university research departments, and technology incubators to cross-pollinate ideas and provide solutions. Founded in 2000, the company has become a leader in expert-sourcing, offering clients such as GlaxoSmithKline, Phillips, Kraft, Unilever, and Xerox access to its network as well as an extensive database of existing solutions that span all industries and technical disciplines.
- Founded in 1999, yet2.com brings together buyers and sellers of technologies so all parties maximize the return on their investments. Yet2.com focuses on later-stage technologies, rather than on ideas.
- TopCoder bills itself as the world's largest competitive software-development community, with more than 175,000 developers representing more than 200 countries. The community builds software for a wide-ranging client base through a competitive, rigorous, standards-based methodology.
- YourEncore connects companies with retired scientists and engineers, who provide expertise within the life sciences, consumer sciences, food sciences, specialty materials, and aerospace and defense industries. YourEncore was founded in 2003, with P&G and Eli Lilly as initial clients and the mandate to tap into an underutilized asset: the growing number of retired and veteran scientists.

The Essential Element of Trust

Trust is fundamental to open innovation. It comes at many levels—internally as well as externally. As you move toward open innovation, you should begin to look into two questions:

1. What does it take for you to trust others?
2. How do you convince your external stakeholders to build trust in you and your company, and then start forging strong relationships?

The necessity of building trust as a basis for successful open innovation means that it is more relevant to look at the people side of innovation than to concentrate on processes, and it also brings more power to the people who really drive innovation within a company.

Why? Trust is first and foremost established between people and then perhaps between organizations. Trust is a personal thing, and the innovation leaders who understand this are suddenly in a much better position with regard to making things happen and creating an interesting and challenging career.

What are the barriers against building trust and relationships with stakeholders in your ecosystem?

- Most organizational structures foster an internal rather than an external perspective.
- Most companies view external partners as people paid to deliver a specific service rather than a source of co-creation and open innovation.
- Most companies are more focused on protecting their own knowledge and intellectual property rather than opening up and exploring new opportunities. They play defense rather than offense. This should not come as a surprise as one of the main objectives for corporate lawyers is to minimize risk, and it is fair to say that opening up to the outside world increases the risk element.
- Forging strong relationships takes time and personal commitment. We are just too busy to make it happen, and it does not help that most companies do not provide the necessary time, resources, and encouragement to make this happen.

What should you do to foster an organizational mindset that supports the building of trust?

The most difficult situation faced by most innovation leaders working with open innovation is that they are alone. This is a new way of doing things, and it will develop many corporate antibodies who just want things to stay as they have always been.

This is a very normal reaction; many people feel threatened by something that is new and doesn't seem to match what has led the organization to success in the past. So you do not get much support for this new way of thinking from anyone within your company. They might see that this could be interesting, but once they begin to understand that you have to make significant changes in the way you are dealing with external stakeholders, they begin to raise obstacles rather than see opportunities.

You need to recruit enough people with a proper mindset to lay the foundation for trust, which in turn makes everyone accept that strong relationships are the key to business success in the future.

Unfortunately, it is my experience that few companies have laid this foundation, and this will not happen unless you become successful in recruiting the right people with the right mindset. You can more or less just forget about processes and concepts because, when it comes to open innovation, it is the mindset that matters the most. If you get the mindset right, the implementation of processes will be so much easier to deal with.

⚸⚹ Key Chapter Takeaways

- The form open innovation takes varies dramatically from company to company.
- Open innovation is about bridging internal and external resources throughout the entire innovation process to make innovation happen.
- The real differentiator in the various forms of open innovation is the level of involvement from external partners, customers, or suppliers.
- Open innovation is about integrating external partners in the entire innovation process.

(continued)

- User-driven innovation is highly related to open innovation, but it has to go further in bringing external partners to the whole innovation process to become open innovation.
- User-driven and open innovation can be a powerful combination.
- The chief benefits of open innovation are to:
  - Speed the development of new products and services and thus increase revenues and market share.
  - Shorten time to market for new products and services and accelerate profits.
  - Reduce direct spending on R&D.
  - Improve the success rate of new products and services.[2]
- Three fundamental questions must be answered before embarking on a journey toward open innovation:
  1. What will open innovation do to your business model?
  2. How will your organizational chart change to accommodate open innovation?
  3. What does this mean to my role as manager or leader?
- Trust is fundamental to open innovation.
- The need to build trust as a basis for successful open innovation means that it is more relevant to look at the people side of innovation than concentrate on processes, and it also brings more power to the people who really drive innovation within a company.

CHAPTER

3

How to Approach Open Innovation

Many people believe open innovation is the Holy Grail, and they just jump aboard without asking that all-important question that I mentioned back in Chapter 1: Why is open innovation relevant to your company, its present situation, and its mission and vision? If you haven't answered this question thoroughly, you need to bring your feet back on the ground and remember that open innovation is just a tool, not a goal. The goal is to grow your company and make a profit.

You should also have in mind that open innovation is just a piece of the overall innovation strategy and it may not even work for all companies. So you have to start out by asking this question: Why do we want open innovation?

An answer to the why question should show an understanding of how open innovation can be an important part of the general innovation strategy, which in turn needs to be highly aligned with the overall corporate strategy. But many companies don't even have an overall innovation strategy, much less a specific open innovation strategy that links with it.

The benefit of having an innovation strategy is that it sets a direction for your efforts. This also allows you to better define open innovation in the terms of the company. Innovation and— even more so—open innovation can be defined in so many different ways. Companies need to find their own definitions as P&G,

General Mills, and other companies have done. (See interview at end of this chapter for General Mills' definition.)

Once the why and the definition are in place, it becomes easier to work out a strategy and implement it. You also need to focus on the people issue. A paradigm shift like this requires that people change their mindset and obtain new skills. The key thing here is the ability to view innovation in more holistic terms. Innovation should be about more than just core products and services, and it should involve as many business functions as possible rather than just R&D and Sales & Marketing. When I do talks or sessions at companies, I often meet the usual suspects. By far the largest contingency comes from R&D supplemented with a few market-oriented people. Where are the guys from procurement, supply chain, or finance? I take it as a sign of a strong innovation culture when multiple business functions participate in innovation initiatives. Unfortunately, this does not happen very often.

Elements of an Open Innovation Culture

In my 15inno community on LinkedIn, Chris Thoen, a R&D director at P&G, started a spirited discussion by asking which elements are needed to create an open innovation culture. The community suggested that open innovation requires these elements:

- People who can manage relationships with customers and partners. This requires agile and flexible people who have the soft skills of emotional intelligence—fundamental social skills such as self-awareness, self-fulfillment, and empathy—in addition to traditional intelligence skills.
- Willingness to accept that not all the smart people work in your department or even for your company, and a corresponding willingness to find and work with smart people both inside and outside the company.
- Willingness to help employees build the knowledge and understanding of how an idea or technology becomes a profitable business, perhaps by developing a job-rotation program that could even engage partners and customers.
- Understanding that failures represent opportunities to learn, and a willingness to reward those efforts and that way of

learning. Failure is a fact of life for companies that pursue innovation seriously, and a leader's response has a huge effect on company culture and, therefore, on future projects.

- Dismissing NIH (Not Invented Here). If we make the best use of internal and external ideas, we will win. We don't need to own everything ourselves and keep it under tight wraps. We should profit from others' use of our innovation process, and we should buy others' intellectual property whenever it advances our own business model.
- Willingness to strive for balance between internal and external R&D. External R&D can create significant value; internal R&D is needed to claim some portion of that value.
- Willingness to be a risk taker rather than being risk averse, while using common sense to balance the risk level.
- Accepting that open innovation does raise intellectual property issues. Your legal team can either choose to play offense or defense. Hopefully, they'll adopt a constructive approach that supports progress toward the company's business development goals.
- Understanding that open innovation requires open communication. Work around the confidentiality and intellectual property rights issues to create an environment built on trust.
- Not needing to always be first. Building a better business model is better than getting to market first.

Finally, recognize that it is no longer enough to just be a good project manager, researcher, or engineer—or leader. As you will learn in this book, open innovation not only requires a different mindset; it also requires new skills that include the following:

- Holistic point of view—the X-vision.
  If you want to create significant innovation, you must be able to work across business functions and with many types of innovation to turn ideas into profitable products, services, or business methods. I call this X-vision. This is actually more of a mindset rather than a skill, but it's extremely important to develop.
- Networking.
  Open innovation is all about networking, so the ability to build a networking culture is an essential role of an innovation

leader as companies move more toward open innovation. See Chapter 15 for an in-depth discussion on this topic.

- Making an effective elevator pitch.

   As your company reaches out to other organizations, you need to be able to craft compelling messages to the people you want to influence. This also applies to the internal stakeholders who can make or break the projects you work on. I'll cover this topic in depth in Chapter 16.

- Managing stakeholders.

   You do not need to have everyone on your side, but you need to generate adequate support to champion your ideas and enough leverage to overcome major hurdles. See Chapter 8 for more on this.

In the chapters ahead you will learn how to develop an internal culture that embraces and rewards open innovation and that supports your personal objectives of being a great innovation leader.

Tough Questions and Great Answers—General Mills Steps Up to the Open Innovation Plate

At a first glance, the G-WIN initiative by General Mills looks just like the many other open innovation portals that are popping up right now.

So rather than just giving my two cents on this, I did an interview with Jeff Bellairs, who is director of General Mills Worldwide Innovation Network, to get a better understanding of the whys and hows of this initiative.

This turned into a great learning experience that I would like to share with others. I kicked off the interview by telling Jeff that I was kind of neutral on their project. Some things looked good and others not so good. I also mentioned that a press release they'd recently sent out on the project and the portal itself raised several questions.

I asked quite direct and candid questions, and I did not really expect much from his answers. So the open and informative feedback given by Jeff Bellairs was a quite a pleasant surprise. The interview went like this:

Can you explain the WHY behind this initiative?

Bellairs: We have learned an incredible amount in the more than four years that we have had a dedicated connected-innovation program and our new web site reflects much of those insights. One of the key things we discovered was that we needed a more efficient way to match our top business needs with the talent who had the potential to solve those problems and meet those needs.

We believe that through our alpha partnership with inno360, we are well on our way to developing a connection workbench that will accelerate our efforts to clearly articulate our business needs and identify needed talent. The following are key web site enhancements based on our learning:

- Clearly articulated needs.
- Nonconfidential submission process.
- Timely reviews.
- Invitation to join G-WIN network so that we push needs to individuals with the right skills and interest.

How does General Mills define open innovation?

Bellairs: We actually prefer the term *connected innovation.* At its core, it's all about connecting more effectively to smart people who can help us meet our business needs most effectively. The connection could be with colleagues, suppliers, other food companies, or perhaps companies in entirely different industries. Our program is focused on building the tools and processes needed to connect most effectively across this spectrum of possibilities.

What is the link from this Initiative to your Innovation Strategy? And how does this help your overall Corporate Strategy?

Bellairs: Our innovation strategy is to build a rich pipeline of new products and product enhancements that deliver high levels of taste, health, and convenience to consumers. Our connected-innovation program seeks to enhance and accelerate those efforts by leveraging the global pool of scientists, engineers, and other creative individuals who can solve technical problems and supply needed capabilities.

Which actions have you taken to become the preferred partner of choice within your industry? My early observation is that the G-WIN portal does not really seem to focus on others than General Mills.

(continued)

Bellairs: The partner-of-choice moniker is earned by consistent actions and by demonstrated leadership in the open innovation area. We believe that we have the needed elements in place to earn that title and are well on our way. We have:

- A dedicated External Partner Development group focused on building creative business models and partnering relationships so that both General Mills and our partners receive value. Our goal is to create mutually beneficial relationships and to reward our partners equitably for their contributions.
- A team of innovation entrepreneurs dedicated to each of our businesses who triage submission on a timely basis and seamlessly integrate external components into development projects.
- A dedicated centralized connected innovation team that is developing new tools and methodologies, and sharing much of that work through publications and speaking engagements.

We have developed a portfolio of successful products, have a growing list of awards and external recognitions, and, most importantly, have a number of partners who are seeing tangible rewards from partnering with General Mills.

On this, I would like to know more about which actions you have taken to make the connection between external and internal resources as smooth as possible in the introduction as well as the integration phases?

Bellairs: Great question. About a year ago we took a retrospective look at many of our connected-innovation projects, paying special attention to those where there had been a speed bump along the way. We learned that although we have a well-grooved process for commercializing internally developed products, we were missing a similar process for on-boarding externally sourced technologies and products.

Our answer has been to establish an External Speed Team, a cross-functional team that meets every other week to openly discuss projects, share insights, and to make sure the appropriate communications are taking place.

In addition, we launched our innovation-entrepreneur program so that we have dedicated connected-innovation resources (or people) in each of our business divisions. Those individuals have a number of responsibilities, one of them assuring effective integration of externally sourced capabilities into the business pipeline of initiatives.

The press release mentions on G-WIN that "partners who help the company achieve its innovation goals can benefit from General Mills' resources, scale and credibility in the marketplace to advance their own business." Can you elaborate a bit on this?

Bellairs: With sales of almost $16 billion, General Mills is the sixth-largest food company in the world and a company with tremendous scale. We have a portfolio of brands that are among the most trusted and respected in the food industry and a dedicated sales force who can assure that we get immediate distribution on new products. These are critical elements needed for success and elements that most entrepreneurs don't have access to. When we approach a partnering opportunity, we work to build synergistic relationships where our unique capabilities supplement and enhance the capabilities of the partner. We believe that the barriers to entry are low in the food business but that the barriers to attaining scale are high. Our resources and capabilities can reduce those barriers.

Which steps have you taken toward building ecosystems of partners working together to develop new products, solutions, ideas, and technologies?

Bellairs: We often talk about the four levels of connected innovation. The first three being effective internal collaboration, collaboration with suppliers and other trusted partners, and collaboration with new partners. We talk about the fourth level being one of building new collaboration models, and in that area we have a number of efforts underway. Two examples are:

1. Consortia—We are actively experimenting with consortia models that pool resources and insights, create scale, and mitigate risks in a project in the sustainability area.
2. We are building an ecosystem of partners whose combined skills will enable us to meet a need in the health and wellness space. As we mapped the existing ecosystem we learned that no one partner could solve the problem alone, but that by bringing the companies together with the right focus and vision, we believe we are well on the way toward a breakthrough technology.

The G-WIN project seems to focus on R&D within General Mills. How do you involve other types of innovation and business functions as well?

(continued)

Bellairs: Our open innovation program began within the R&D organization. As our program has grown, it has spread across much of our organization. We firmly believe that we can be even more successful as we tap into the smart people outside of General Mills who can help us drive our businesses forward, whether they impact our R&D, operations, marketing, or some other aspect of our business.

What were the biggest obstacles internally on this project?

Bellairs: The biggest challenge has been simplifying the very complex process of articulating needs and matching those needs to key players in the global talent pool. Our goal has been to create a connection workbench that our developers can use to architect new connections. We are delighted with the thought leadership and talent at inno360, and believe that we are making great progress toward building that simple, intuitive workbench.

Upon receiving these answers from Jeff, I e-mailed back: "This is great stuff! It gives a much better picture of your open innovation efforts and I really like several of your initiatives. Why did you not include some of this information on the web site? I am especially thinking about your answers related to partner of choice and how to connect internal and external resources. If I were on the other end, I would be pleased to know you had such initiatives."

To this, Jeff replied: "The reason some of this information isn't on the web site yet is that we're still evolving our web site, having a redesign planned for early next calendar year. We wanted to get the word out on the new capabilities of the innovation portal now, rather than wait until the full redesign. So we appreciate and welcome your thoughts and input on the type of information that would be most useful to outside partners."

I like the fact that General Mills acknowledges that they are still learning and that they are brave enough to start learning on the fly in the real world and get the feedback needed to improve their initiative. Kudos to General Mills on this as well as for their insights on how to approach open innovation.

🔑 Key Chapter Takeaways

- Your answer to the question of why your company should try open innovation needs to address how open innovation can be an important part of the general innovation strategy, which in turn needs to be highly aligned with the overall corporate strategy.
- The paradigm shift entailed with open innovation requires that people change their mindset and obtain new skills.
- Innovation should be about more than just core products and services, and it should involve as many business functions as possible rather than just R&D and sales & marketing.
- The elements of open innovation include:
  - People who can manage relationships with customers and partners.
  - Willingness to accept that not all the smart people work in your department or even for your company, and a corresponding willingness to find and work with smart people both inside and outside the company.
  - Willingness to help employees build the knowledge and understanding of how an idea or technology becomes a profitable business, perhaps by developing a job rotation program that could even engage partners and customers.
  - Understanding that failures represent opportunities to learn, and a willingness to reward those efforts and that way of learning.
  - Dismissing NIH (not invented here).
  - Willingness to strive for balance between internal and external R&D.
  - Willingness to be a risk taker rather than being risk averse, while using common sense to balance the risk level.
  - Accepting that open innovation does raise intellectual property issues. Your legal team can either choose to play offense or defense.
- Understanding that open innovation requires open communication. Work around the confidentiality and intellectual property rights issues to create an environment built on trust.
- Not needing to always be first. Building a better business model is better than getting to market first.
- Open innovation not only requires a different mindset; it also requires new skills that include:
  - Holistic point of view—the X-vision.
  - Networking.
  - Making an effective elevator pitch.
  - Managing stakeholders.

4

First Things First

When you start on the path to building an open innovation organization, it's critical to understand that you will only get one-and-a-half chances to do this thing right.

Why one-and-a-half? If you cannot build momentum on your first attempt, you may be given another shot at it. But this time you won't be starting with a clean slate, so your odds of success will be less than the first time around. In other words, you will only be given half a chance because the disbelief created by failing at the first try will make any second attempt a serious uphill battle.

In this chapter, we look at the critical first steps you should take to help ensure success on that all-important first try. Taking these steps will build a strong backbone for your initiative by overcoming the people-related hurdles that impede innovation success in many organizations. (The advice in this chapter is applicable for any innovation strategy, not just open innovation efforts.)

These steps are:

- Establish a clear mandate, a strong strategic purpose, and an ideation theme.
- Conduct a stakeholder analysis.
- Develop a communication strategy.
- Build a common language.
- Include organizational approaches that achieve TBX (T=top down; B=bottom up, X=across).
- Strive to *be* innovative instead of working to *become* innovative.

What Is Your Mandate for Open Innovation?

For you to stand any chance of getting things right the first time, employees must believe company leaders are serious about a transformation to an open innovation culture. Is it just talk, or have the innovation leaders been given a strong mandate to make real change? And are the innovation leaders up for the challenge? The answers to these key questions become apparent to employees very rapidly. Any dissonance between the open innovation mandate and objective, and the reality of how things are actually being done, cannot be hidden.

The executives and senior innovation leaders must develop an intention in the form of a strategic purpose, but they must also define the mandate given to the innovation leaders. A clearly given mandate can help work out the inevitable internal conflicts with regard to resources and authority given to the innovation team.

The mandate should be easy to communicate to stakeholders, who will be involved in reaching the intent or purpose. The mandate should

- Lay out the resources and authority given to the innovation team.
- Clarify how potential conflicts are to be handled.
- Encourage stakeholders to solve problems on issues, such as resource allocation and commitment, without involving the executives.

The innovation leaders must get full support from the executives. If middle managers sense that innovation leaders do not have executive support, they will tend to focus on their own agendas rather than on what is best for the company. In such cases executives need to send strong signals that they are personally committed to the open innovation initiative. Executives may need to show their commitment in showdowns with individuals and groups. Jørgen Mads Clausen, former CEO at Danfoss, was very good at taking managers aside and looking them straight in the eye while telling them that he really believed in this innovation initiative and that he hoped the manager shared this approach.

Innovation leaders must also educate executives on open innovation and, more importantly, must make the consequences of executive decisions very clear.

Innovation issues are not easy for innovation leaders and executives. A few years ago, I had an interesting talk with an innovation leader at an international producer of high-end goods. The company had relied on a stable product portfolio for many years, and despite that success, knew it had to look beyond incremental innovation. This company needed to work on paradigm shifts that included a stronger focus on services and solutions rather than on just products.

For this they brought in a great innovation leader who quickly built a team of people with varied backgrounds and competencies. It was a good match between incremental and radical innovation, but inevitably the different mindsets led to many clashes.

The innovation leader had to educate the CEO on his ideas and mindset. That process went well, but the innovation leader and his team continued to clash with other parts of the organization. The innovation leader brought this up with the CEO, and he was a bit surprised to receive this response: "Bob, I like what you are doing, and I really want to support your work. You know that. However, if your initiatives cause too much trouble, I need to listen to our core people. They are the guys who bring in our revenues and profits, and we need this. Try to work this out in a subtle manner."

The clear message was that, if there is too much trouble, the CEO would have to kick out the innovation leader with short notice to satisfy the other guys. Unfortunately, unlike this case, many innovation leaders do not have a clear mandate from their executives. This can cause bad situations, and it definitely makes the job of an innovation leader even harder.

The Innovation Strategy and Strategic Purposes

As mentioned in the previous chapter, innovation initiatives at their best build from an innovation strategy that is highly aligned with the overall corporate strategy. What should an innovation strategy look like? It can come in many different forms because it needs to reflect the company itself.

I definitely like the innovation intent created by Grundfos, one of the world's leading pump manufacturers. Check out this description taken from a document entitled Gundfos Challenge Assignment 2009:

> At Grundfos we have successfully achieved many of our targets and therefore we have recently reviewed our long-term business perspective by trying to look 15–20 years ahead. This led to the

statement of the Grundfos Innovation Intent. It represents a guiding star that will bring focus to our long-term innovation efforts and make sure the company is heading in the right direction. The Innovation Intent embraces three challenges, all of which every major concept Grundfos launches over the next 20–30 years should meet:

- CONCERN: Put sustainability first.
- CARE: Be there for a growing world.
- CREATE: Pioneer New Technologies.

In other words, Grundfos will establish a substantial position in the growing markets by delivering superior sustainable solutions and offerings based on technology, the world has not yet seen. Perfectly aligned with our core values—being responsible, thinking ahead, and innovating—the Innovation Intent is a clear and bold statement of where and how Grundfos wants to develop its business. It is the ambition, that in 2025:

- Grundfos employs 75,000 people globally—today the number is 18,000.
- 50 percent of our growth is coming from technology platforms that were not invented in 2007.
- One-third of our turnover comes from other products than pumps.
- We are still no. 1 in circulators and a specialist in sustainable solutions for housing.
- We are specialists in selling directly to end-users within selected industrial segments and utilities.
- We gravitate around local centres of excellence tapping into knowledge bases wherever they are.
- We have become experts in translating user needs into new products and business concepts.
- We are the first-choice workplace for the best and the brightest.

Besides innovation work at the core, the company test[s] new possibilities in Grundfos New Business, which develops projects aimed at ensuring the limited resources of the earth will suffice for a rapidly growing population with increasing spending power, without destroying the environment.[1]

I like this link between the overall corporate strategy and innovation, and I definitely look forward to following Grundfos in the future. Some of my blog readers felt this was more of a vision than a strategy, and perhaps they're right. But I think that whatever label you put on it, the key point is that Grundfos has set some direction for their long-term innovation. In this case, I believe the innovation intent can serve as inspiration to others on how to craft an innovation intent/strategy/vision.

One of the most often-cited examples of a general strategic purpose that inspired great things is John F. Kennedy's declaration: "I believe that this nation should commit itself to achieving the goal, before this decade is out, of landing a man on the Moon and returning him safely to Earth." This objective galvanized, not just NASA, but a whole nation behind the effort to beat the Soviet Union in the space race.

Not every organization is involved in innovation efforts as grandiose as sending people to the moon, but stating clearly up front what it is you hope to accomplish is important nonetheless. Today, P&G says that their goal with open innovation is to become the preferred partner of choice within their given industry on open innovation and collaboration. Here are some other and more general examples of strategic purposes that I have encountered in companies I have worked with or researched over the past years:

Danfoss:

- To identify and develop new ventures that create significant growth and/or strategic advantages.
- To spot and develop talent.
- To change the culture and to establish intrapreneurship as the fourth career path.

Intel:

- Foster and encourage innovation and creative thinking.
- Challenge the status quo and embrace change.
- Provide a challenging work environment.

Grundfos:

- Experiment with and develop toward future organizational paradigms.
- Create new career paths for Grundfos managers.

Notice that in each case, a portion of the language focuses on people-related aspects of the organization, such as shifting the corporate culture or developing new career paths. This helps employees answer the key question of "What's in it for me?" In the end innovation needs to be about making money and profits, but this will not happen if you shortcut the people aspect. Innovative companies understand this, and it should be a key lesson for all executives and innovation leaders.

Generating On-Target Ideas by Having an Ideation Theme

Along with your strategic purpose, you should also use ideation themes to frame and focus your idea-generating activities toward a desired outcome. Here's why this is so important. When I talk with innovation leaders about generating ideas, I often say that getting ideas is never the issue. You have plenty of ideas within your organization and even more ideas available if you start to open up to external channels. If you do not think you have enough ideas, it is usually because you are not looking in the right places or do not feel that the ideas are good enough. It is often the latter, so the issue is more about quality than quantity.

How do you find the ideas that really matter? Too many companies make the mistake of not properly structuring their search for ideas. They fail to establish a scope or theme for idea generation that will prompt ideas in areas that match the organization's innovation goals. As a result they have no filter with which to evaluate and select the ideas with real potential.

In other words, the biggest mistake you can make when it comes to idea generation is to tell people that anything goes. Use that approach, and you'll be buried in ideas without having a clear idea of what to with them. This is especially true when you begin asking the outside world for ideas. You'll be hearing from people who may have little or no real understanding of your business. Without giving them some guidance about what specific areas for which you're interested in innovation, you're apt to get an awful lot of chaff and perhaps not much of any real value.

By being more focused and setting up a filtering process, you can quickly evaluate the ideas, deciding that one is pretty much what we're looking for, one isn't a match for our theme at all, or another is somewhere in between. Without such a process, you'll be swamped with ideas that are likely to go nowhere.

Your ideation theme should be driven by your innovation strategy. It should be clear and fresh, something that will excite people and motivate them to do some in-depth thinking about areas they may not have focused on before.

For example, in a stroke of prescient thinking, the CEO of Danfoss challenged the participants in their first business plan competition (which I'll discuss in depth in the bonus chapter), to think of business ideas for Danfoss if the price of oil reached more than $100—which it did four years later. In year two of its business plan competition, Hewlett-Packard stipulated that all ideas had to be new businesses that could operate in the Web 2.0 environment. Being this focused and clear on what types of ideas you're looking for is like using a sniper scope rather than a shotgun.

Here's another example. In this case, the company has outlined its objectives to the whole world and asked people outside the company to participate in innovation. In its 2005 annual report, Toyota described its vision and the philosophy that guides its technology development initiatives. Here, in part, is what it said:

> Under the vision of "Zeronize," we are persistently seeking to eliminate the negative aspects of car society, such as environmental problems, traffic accidents, and congestion, while fully maximizing, under the vision of "Maxi-mize"-ing, the positive aspects, including fun, comfort, and convenience.[2]

Then in 2007, Toyota North America launched an ad campaign called "Why Not," based on three themes, including environmental commitment, economic impact, and social responsibility. In 2009, it launched a user-driven idea- harvesting campaign through a web site at www.toyotawhynot.com. At this site, Toyota asks consumers for ideas on how to innovate within areas such as safety (safer communities), water (reduce consumption), land (preserve public land), air (cleaner air), energy (save energy), and communities (bring people together). The web site tells people that:

> At Toyota, we are passionate about creating new ways to improve our environment and help enrich society. We rely on continuous improvement to propel us forward. But we want to

(continued)

know what inspires you. We've created an interactive space for you to share your innovative thinking and build your own community. So, explore, create, and contribute. Together, we can make a real difference.

I really like how Toyota has linked the idea-harvesting campaign to a corporate-innovation intent and to an overall advertising campaign. Furthermore, Toyota is not just asking for any idea; they are being specific in what they are looking for.

Stakeholder Analysis

The innovation team must get an overview of the internal and external stakeholders, and analyze the pros and cons of the open innovation initiative for these people. Who will be affected by the open innovation intention? What issues bother these people? How can the innovation leaders create a value proposition that will make the stakeholders support the initiative?

One approach is to create a stakeholder map that identifies all the various groups, then develop specific value propositions for each group. Don't forget to focus on informal influencers, that is, people with a disproportionate level of influence. Find these people and win them over to your cause, and it will be easier to build the innovation DNA.

Communication Strategy

Strong communication programs are important at any time within an organization, but never more so than when open innovation is your goal. Without a good communications strategy, your odds for success during your one-and-a-half chances do not look good. To move forward, people need to know where to go and how to get there. Knowing the strategic goals motivates people and builds a collective sense of purpose. So put a communications plan in place before you even start. Make sure you take every opportunity to turn good news into a story that can work internally as well as externally. The latter is especially useful if recruitment is a serious issue. Who does not want to work for an organization that is perceived as highly innovative?

Senior executives should actively communicate about the importance of your open innovation effort and their strong support for it. You should also develop specific communication points of view to your stakeholder groups. It's even better if these points of view are aligned with the value propositions.

Common Language

A key objective of your communication strategy is to develop a shared language about open innovation—and innovation in general—within your company. When everyone uses the same language, it is significantly easier to frame the issues in ways that everyone can understand and relate to. As reported in the *MIT Sloan Management Review* article, "Institutionalizing Innovation," Intel Corp.'s response to competitive threats at the low end of the microprocessor business in the late 1990s illustrates the value of a shared language.

Clayton Christensen, a Harvard Business School professor and founder of Innosight, a consulting and training firm, made numerous appearances at Intel to educate hundreds of managers on the principles and language of disruptive innovation. Intel subsequently slowed the advances of disruptive competitors by introducing its own low-cost chip. Christensen recalls that Intel CEO Andy Grove told him, "You know, the model didn't give us any answers to any of the problems, but it gave us a common language and a common way to frame the problem so that we could reach consensus around counterintuitive courses of action."[1]

Grundfos New Business Development, which develops new business areas outside the core pump business of the Danish industrial company, Grundfos, had a good approach for imbuing an entire organization with a shared language of innovation. In one instance they brought in Mark Cavender (www.chasminstitute.com), who is an expert on go-to-market strategies based on *Crossing the Chasm,* for a full week—not just for one session or one workshop. During this week, the head of Grundfos New Business hosted workshops and sessions for his colleagues and the staff of portfolio companies as well as for executives, managers, and employees from the core business. This makes it simple for him to refer to concepts in *Crossing the Chasm* to the stakeholders in the future and thus get his ideas through quickly and easily.

Grundfos NBD does the same thing with other consultants and gurus, as they try to send as many people as possible to conferences and educational programs. In this way they look for new knowledge and also networking opportunities that can help them frame a common language with which to talk about innovation. This should be an important factor in setting up internal educational programs.

TBX(O)

You need to have three organizational approaches in mind when developing your company's open innovation DNA:

- T (Top Down)—Get executives on board and require their personal commitment to the open innovation activities. Without executive support, no change occurs.
- B (Bottom Up)—Value creation begins with people—one by one, team by team. Nothing happens unless you get employees engaged and involved. Also, going back to the one-and-a-half chances you have to make things work, it is important that ideas, feedback, and other input from the employees and external partners are taken seriously by the innovation leaders. If ideas just seem to fall into a sinkhole, never to re-emerge, or if leaders are not able to commit resources to any ideas, you will lose the trust of the employees and outside partners.
- X (Across)—The biggest challenges will come from the middle managers placed across the organization, because they have a narrow focus on their own profit-and-loss responsibility. They do not see the full picture and, thus, will not give up resources when doing so does not benefit them in the short run, even though it is the right thing for the company in the long run. If not dealt with appropriately and effectively, they can bring open innovation, indeed, innovation of any type, to a grinding halt.

For open innovation, we also need to add another factor: O (Outsiders). External partners will bring knowledge, skills, experience—and demands—to your organization. You need to be prepared for the ways in which this outside influence will affect the development of the innovation DNA in your company.

Be Innovative Rather than Strive to Become Innovative

I once did a workshop at a company trying to establish processes for innovation. This company is in much better shape than others, because it is run by entrepreneurs who like spinouts that offer many opportunities for employees who have the drive and capabilities needed for creating new ventures.

Nevertheless, the management team had spent much energy on one big question: How do we become an innovative company, and how do we convince our employees that we can reach that goal? I invited them to turn this question around: What if it is not a question of becoming, but one of being? The company already had initiatives that would qualify it as being innovative, so the foundation for this shift was in place. A better question: What should the next steps be?

- **It begins at the top.**

    You cannot convince anyone unless you are convinced yourself. The management team really needs to believe in their own innovation capabilities. Keep it simple; discover just a few capabilities on which everyone agrees that the innovation level is high, then use this common understanding as the platform for the other steps.

- **Let proof follow perception.**

    Perception is everything. Once the management team discovers their real innovation capabilities, make a survey or conduct some other benchmarking exercise that turns this newly found perception into proof.

- **Offer real initiatives.**

    Now, it is time to step up with real initiatives that convince employees, customers, and other stakeholders, including external partners, that their opinions and contributions to the innovation process are truly valued. Such initiatives could range from simple idea boxes to 24-hour innovation camps to business plan competitions and networks for internal innovators and potential external innovation partners. The real challenge is to listen and actually do something with the results on a regular basis. It could also be open innovation portals such as Dell's Ideastorm, MyStarbucksIdea, P&G's Connect & Develop, or it could be events such as Intuit's Entrepreneur Day in which a select group of entrepreneurs, startups, and small but more-established companies got the opportunity to meet and talk with a broad group of senior Intuit leaders.

- **Make it public.**

  There is nothing more satisfying for employees than reading about their own capabilities, or even better, having family, friends and business contacts read about them. So work out great stories, and let the world know how good you are. Then your employees will begin to believe.

Again, this is very much about perception rather than facts. Manage the perceptions right, and the reality will follow. Your company will be on track to have innovation capabilities integrated into its DNA.

Pumps Today; Radical Innovation for the Future!

Mads Prebensen is Group Senior Vice President responsible for Grundfos New Business, which works with radical innovation projects outside Grundfos's core business—pumps. In this interview, he talks about how Grundfos New Business works with radical innovation.

A few years ago Grundfos decided to accelerate its new business development efforts. Why?

Prebensen: Grundfos had always done new-business development as a staff function, and we have more than 20 years of experience working with radical innovation. However, many of the radical innovation projects failed or did not reach the market with strong enough impact. They did not have enough commercial focus (because) they were often driven by technology people.

The accumulated investments made it necessary to rethink the strategy, and it was decided to invest more in the staffing around these fairly radical projects. Besides adding resources, we also restructured, and today Grundfos New Business is a separate legal entity within the group.

The board also realized that it would be necessary to prepare for a future in which the pump business might begin to fade. We must continuously redefine ourselves, and that is the main reason for scaling up our radical innovation projects.

Until recently, our new business development activities were inside out; they were based on the core pump activities. It was difficult to develop radical ideas in this structure. Our board understood that running radical innovation projects within the core activities could not work. That machine is too streamlined and focused on the daily operations. With Grundfos New Business we have a platform for radical innovation where new projects can be given a future out of the core and with a structure that fits their needs.

You are leading this new unit. What has been the biggest challenge?

Prebensen: I have been the head of this unit for two and a half years now. In this period, my key objective has been to make radical innovation more successful than in the past. We need to create solid returns on our investments.

Early on, I realized the radical innovation projects should be lifted into our new structure and we should also develop new HR paradigms, such as share ownerships. Today, we have general managers instead of project managers on our more mature projects; these people are quite similar to entrepreneurs. Actually, Grundfos New Business looks very much like a venture capital company in many ways.

The biggest challenge was not in convincing the board and the core that we needed this new structure and mindset. The real challenge came with the practical implementation. During board-level presentations you do not have time to dive into details, which meant we had to fight two battles during the implementation.

First, we needed to make sure the board—and the top management team—followed through on their overall vision, even though they also had to balance the issues and needs of the core as well as of Grundfos New Business.

We still had to work out many issues with core staff functions on topics such as recruitment for specific people and new compensation schemes. It was difficult (because) they were used to do things differently. It was a learning process for all of us. It still is.

Grundfos New Business decided to develop projects that are quite different from the core business. Can you give us a couple of examples?

(continued)

Prebensen: Our projects all operate in different markets or with different business models than do our core activities.

A good example is NoNox, which develops products and services based on a digital pump technology. It has been adapted by the automotive industry, and the contacts already secured will make this a big business. NoNox can add a couple of billion (DKK) in revenue in a market where Grundfos has never succeeded before by itself. Furthermore, NoNox has helped us build a name within the automotive industry, and this will provide a lot of industry know-how and insights. Our core activities can learn from this and use this as an inroad to the automotive industry. This is a good example of how a project can give us access to a broader market as well as being a good business by itself.

We have also introduced new business models at Grundfos. An example is BioBooster, an extremely compact biological wastewater pretreatment plant. Originally, Grundfos started this project by developing it as a component that could work in flexible and movable solutions. Unfortunately, the other devices for the solution were not flexible and movable. The customers could not benefit from our innovation. The project came to Grundfos New Business, and we decided to sell, not just the component, but a full package in which the booster is a component. Today, we offer the food industry a complete wastewater plant that can be leased under a build/own/operate agreement if desired. We take full responsibility.

This is a completely new business model for Grundfos. Normally we just sell components. Now we are also making money on operating and owning assets. This can only be done within industries that are not vital to our core, which has to protect its current customers and ecosystem.

We need to develop such new models to reach our future revenue goals. We also need to make sure that core learns from the experiences of Grundfos New Business.

What has been your key lesson on developing such radical projects?

Prebensen: Realize that projects go through phases and that you need the right horses for the right courses. Early in a project lifecycle you often need to develop the technology, which requires one kind of manager. As the project matures, you must shift to people with more of a background in commercialization, who are more entrepreneurial. This shift must be done proactively and ruthlessly.

Key Chapter Takeaways

- You only get one-and-a-half chances to do open innovation right, so you must prepare carefully.
- The key elements that must be put in place before moving forward with an open innovation initiative include:
  - A clear mandate, a strong strategic purpose, and an ideation theme.
  - A stakeholder analysis.
  - A communication strategy.
  - A shared language about innovation in your company.
  - Organizational approaches that achieve TBX (top down, bottom up, and across).
  - Adopt an attitude of striving to *be* innovative vs. working to *become* innovative.
- Your open innovation mandate should:
  - Lay out the resources and authority given to the innovation team.
  - Clarify how potential conflicts are to be handled.
  - Encourage stakeholders to solve problems, such as resource allocation and commitment, without involving executives.
- Make sure your strategic purpose answers this key employee question: "What's in it for me?"
- Establish a scope or theme for idea generation that will prompt ideas in areas that match the organization's innovation goals.
- Bring in the O (outside) factor in addition to TBX.
- Build your company's innovation DNA with real initiatives that convince all stakeholders that their contributions are valued.
- Help employees believe that your company is innovative by sharing great stories.

5

How to Identify and Develop the People Who Drive Open Innovation

I t still happens. I meet with a group of innovation leaders and a discussion opens up on the front end of innovation—how to generate new ideas and projects. Some guy starts talking about his company's new idea-harvesting campaign. It has been a great initiative, and they have gotten more than 600 ideas.

I am not sure whether to laugh or cry. The guy is happy, but he also has revealed that he is a rookie when it comes to innovation. He has not yet learned that the number of ideas is not the most important thing. Yes, you need a large number of ideas in your funnel to assure that you'll get enough good ones, but you should not celebrate just because you have 600 ideas. You should only start getting excited once you have 600 ideas and a clear and quick process that will winnow that number down to about 30 ideas worth exploring further. Even more importantly, you shouldn't really start celebrating until you've been able to match those 30 ideas with the people who can do the hard work of figuring out if and how they can be turned into profitable realities.

Here's what often happens with idea-harvesting campaigns that focus on quantity rather than quality and ignore the paramount importance of the people component of innovation success:

- You get the 600 ideas into your system, but you do not have enough resources to work through all of them.

47

- You start getting inquiries from people who submitted ideas and who are genuinely curious about the next steps. You tell them you will get back to them—within the coming month.
- These same people get back to you again six weeks later. This time they sound more discouraged than enthusiastic. You are still drowning in work, and although you have reviewed all the ideas, you still are not yet sure which ones to bet on. You ask them to come back a month later. This is probably the last time you'll hear from the idea generators, who have lost all hope that something will actually happen with their ideas.
- The next time you put a call out for new ideas, fewer people are willing to take time to participate because the ideas from the first campaign never went anywhere.

Of course, this is exaggerated, but I have heard of enough situations like this to know that it happens more often than you would think. It is not unusual for companies that focus on generating high volumes of ideas through internal and external idea-harvesting campaigns to have issues with sorting and qualifying ideas. Furthermore, such companies often are also unable to attach the right people to the right ideas at the right times. Good people offer up good ideas, only to see them disappear into a black hole, never to emerge again.

Too much focus on the quantity of ideas can also drive your innovation culture in the wrong direction. Most of the ideas you get are from people who just want to contribute to feel innovative. Ideas are free, and it's easy to submit an idea and hope others will follow up and perhaps execute it.

Now these pseudo-idea-generators can consider themselves to be innovative. As they talk with colleagues who also submitted ideas, they are all convinced they work in a company with a well-developed innovation culture. Similarly, if ideas are being brought into the company through an open innovation process, people can say, "See, we're so innovative here that we are even searching the entire world for more great ideas!" But if they looked carefully, they would notice that nothing really has changed, because no process exists for evaluating and moving ideas forward. So you've made some people feel good temporarily, but innovation is not really happening. Repeat this pattern a few times, and that image of a well-developed innovation culture dies.

You need to understand the right order: People first, processes next, then ideas, if you want to build a strong and sustainable innovation culture. This book is not so much about processes and ideas, but it is very much about people, so let's move on with this in mind.

Focus on People

The chief thing you as an innovation leader must realize is that when it comes to making innovation of all types happen, people matter more than ideas.

Take a moment to think about that. Many innovation initiatives fail miserably because their leaders don't understand this simple fact. In fact, it is actually more important to have grade-A people than it is to have a slew of grade-A ideas. Why? Because grade-A people can take a grade-B idea—or perhaps even a grade-C idea—and turn it into a successful reality. Grade-B people, on the other hand, will struggle with even truly great ideas.

There is an ongoing discussion in the venture capital community on which of these two options is best: (1) An outstanding team with an average idea or (2) the best business idea you have ever seen coupled with average guys. If we take this to the corporate world, the big question is whether you have enough available grade-A people within your organization who can take great ideas, whether they come from inside or outside the company, and turn them into reality. A major advantage for large corporations over venture-capital companies is that, in a large corporation, you can switch great people to other projects. Of course, this requires that you have already made the effort to identify and develop great innovation leaders and intrapreneurs. So before you get all fired up about generating a ton of ideas, first figure out how you're going to match those ideas to people who can make things happen.

As you start this work, here's another key point to remember: The skills needed to lead and manage a project within the existing core business—where innovation is likely to be incremental and resources plentiful—are significantly different from the skills needed to overcome the challenges and obstacles that greet almost any new business project, for which resources may be hard to come by and the innovation involved may be significant or even radical. You need to staff new business projects with people who have a mindset and toolbox that match this different challenge.

I recently coached teams working to create new business ideas that had big potential. The managers more or less approached this as if it were business development as usual within core projects; that is, they focused on small incremental steps. They did not understand the dynamics of creating new business development or innovation projects with a high potential. Their biggest mistake was that they assigned ideas to people who had no passion for the specific challenge. However, when it comes to projects involving innovations with radical or breakthrough potential, you need people who have their heart and skin in the game.

You also need different people for the different phases of the innovation process. Just as some entrepreneurs are better at running a company at its very early stage and others are better at helping the business scale once the product is launched, so too are there intrapreneurs who are better suited both in terms of mindset and skills to various phases of the innovation process.

For example, the discovery-innovation-acceleration (D-I-A) model of innovation put forward by the Radical Innovation Group identifies three phases of innovation:

Discovery
- Basic research: internal and external hunting.
- Creation, recognition, elaboration, and articulation of opportunities.

Incubation
- Application development: technical, market learning, market creation, strategic domains.
- Evolving opportunities into business propositions: creating a working hypothesis about what the technology platform could enable in the market, what the market space will ultimately look like, and what the business model will be.

Acceleration
- Early market entry: focus, respond, invest.
- Ramping up the fledgling business to a point where it can stand on its own, relative to other business platforms in the ultimate receiving unit.[1]

This model has been used with success at many companies, which have learned that only a very few people have the skills to move from heading the project in the discovery phase to heading it during the acceleration phase.

Two Kinds of People Needed

All of this raises a question: Should all people within an organization be innovative? That is a frequent discussion topic in my networks. My take is that you try to limit the number of people working with innovation either full time or as significant contributors to about 20 percent of the workforce. The other people really need to take care of the core business that pays for all the new stuff. However, it is important to note that all employees—and, with open innovation, also external stakeholders along the value chain—should be given the chance to get involved with innovation activities, just not at the same time. You want to protect the core from the new business and vice versa.

I have learned that companies need two kinds of people to make innovation initiatives successful. They need *innovation leaders* who focus on the strategic and tactical work of building the internal platform required to develop organizational innovation capabilities—including the culture, the mandate, the processes, and the people. Innovation leaders also often coach, facilitate, and sponsor the second group required for innovation—the *intrapreneurs* who work within the platform created by the innovation leaders to turn ideas and research into real products and services that move the business forward. Thus, in contrast to innovation leaders, intrapreneurs focus on the operational level instead of on strategy, process, and tactics.

I'm defining intrapreneurship as the practice of using entrepreneurial skills without taking on the risks or accountability associated with entrepreneurial activities, that is, starting your own business. Intrapreneurs are employees who behave as entrepreneurs, even though they have the resources and capabilities of the larger firm to draw upon.

Innovation leaders need the ability to read the corporate landscape, and they need to be able to maneuver within corporate politics to secure the necessary internal resources for the innovation projects. They must attend to the issues of many stakeholders, including senior executives, middle managers, and, of course, external partners of all types who are involved in open innovation.

On the other hand, intrapreneurs have an operational role—they must develop a new business that meets the needs of demanding customers. Of course, this also includes coordination with stakeholders from the corporate mothership and other external partners, but intrapreneurs must have a special talent for addressing the needs of paying customers. Intrapreneurs are even rarer within a company than innovation leaders. Based on my experiences, only 1 to 3 percent of a white-collar workforce has what it takes to be a main contributor in turning ideas and research into business.

The number of intrapreneurs is low for two reasons. First, intrapreneurs have the skills and the will necessary to become real entrepreneurs and start their own companies. These people usually do not end up in a large company in the first place. Those who do are often stuck because they followed a traditional career path. They start out in the corporate world with the ambition of starting their own company once they get some experience and earn starting capital. However, once they get used to the security of being in a large company, their entrepreneurial spirit gradually decreases, although it is still much higher than most of their colleagues.

They might also get married and have children, which often dampens the entrepreneurial spirit. Entrepreneurship is very much about uncertainty, and that does not sound appealing to a perhaps risk-adverse spouse worrying about making mortgage payments and building a stable foundation for children. Actually, you are unlikely to become a successful entrepreneur and at the same time enjoy a good family life unless you have strong support from your spouse.

The second reason for the scarce number of intrapreneurs is the corporate environment itself. Intrapreneurs have a constant drive and an innate need to always question the status quo, which often puts them at odds with colleagues. They are at risk of being labeled troublemakers, making their career path within the organization much more difficult.

This often forces them to seek other opportunities. Ideally, they end up in a company that has discovered that troublemakers are not necessarily bad. The lucky ones stay, and they become coveted assets in the effort to develop the company's innovation DNA.

It's important to note that there's a third group of people who work full- or part-time on innovation projects. Let's call them innovation contributors. They are often junior people who are still on a learning curve, or they are experts with specific skills.

Unlike intrapreneurs, they do not take a guiding role in turning ideas into realities; instead they are assigned to projects where they contribute with sheer manpower and/or their specific skills and talents. As such, they are important, but are also easily replaced.

Traits to Look for in Innovation Leaders and Intrapreneurs

The first step in your search for the people who can power the innovation engine of your company is to understand what sets great innovation leaders and intrapreneurs apart. What characteristics will you need to look for as you fill these important slots on your organizational chart?

Fortunately, the traits that make an individual capable of driving change and innovation—abilities that are key definitions of both innovation leaders and intrapreneurs—have become reasonably well defined over the years. These nine key qualities help make innovation leaders and intrapreneurs a different breed of people:

1. Holistic point of view.

    Since their role involves assuring that innovation becomes part of the corporate DNA, innovation leaders need to be capable of analyzing the big picture both in and outside the company. This includes the ability to decipher the internal political landscape that will impact their ability to move innovation forward as well as having a thorough understanding of the outside forces that shape your company's marketplace opportunities. This trait is also helpful for intrapreneurs to have since it will make them better at new business development, too.

2. Talent for networking.

    Innovation requires bringing together people from disparate parts of a business—or even outside the business—to create a united force to drive new ideas forward. Having an innate ability to network is a key asset in making this happen.

    Research done by Rob Cross of the University of Virginia, and Robert J. Thomas and David A. Light of Accenture Institute for High Performance Business, shows that high performers are likely to position themselves at key points in a network and leverage the network around them better when implementing their plans. Also, they found that high performers tend to invest in relationships that extend their expertise and help them avoid learning biases and career traps. Finally, they discovered that high performers value networks and engage in behaviors that lead to high-quality relationships—not just big networks.[2] These are all skills and behaviors you want in innovation leaders and intrapreneurs.

3. Communication skills.

It's impossible to succeed as a change agent without having strong communication skills. Innovation leaders and intrapreneurs need to be clear communicators who can persuade and inspire other people, including those who are reluctant to embrace change. Innovation leaders and intrapreneurs serve as role models for the openness that is required for an innovative corporate culture.

4. Optimism.

They tend to see opportunities rather than problems, and rather than being intimidated by challenges, they are invigorated because they believe they have the ability to overcome any obstacle. Setbacks that would cause others to fold their tents don't shake the faith of these optimists; they are confident in their ability to succeed at anything they set out to do.

5. Passion and drive.

These people want to change the world! This passion fuels the drive needed to overcome any roadblocks that get in their way. However, if senior executives don't share this passion and the corporate culture doesn't support it, true innovators will move on, seeking a company where their passion is encouraged instead of thwarted. Their drive makes them like a piece of cork floating in the ocean. No matter how rough the waters get, they will rise to the surface again and again.

6. Curiosity.

People who are passionate about a subject are also curious about it. They are in a constant learning mode, always wanting to stay ahead of the curve when it comes to knowing about trends and new developments. True innovators also understand that lessons from one arena can often be used to drive innovation in another, so they usually do not confine their learning to just their own narrow field.

It's important for them to be curious about the jobs of others. By having an interest in what other people do and how that impacts the organization, innovation leaders in particular are better prepared to help drive change.

7. Belief in change.

Linked to curiosity; folks who are happy with the status quo or who don't thrive in the chaos that change often entails will not do well in these important roles.

8. A sense of urgency.

Harvard Business School Professor John Kotter, widely regarded as the world's foremost authority on leadership and change, argues in his most recent book, *A Sense of Urgency*, that true change only occurs within companies if leaders are able to instill a sense of urgency throughout the organization. Getting people to move beyond complacency requires an ability to communicate both to the head (through making the business case for change) and the heart (through storytelling that reaches the emotions.)

This is not a skill everyone has. Finding people with an innate sense of urgency—who are able to see the opportunities lying behind many of today's business challenges and who are excited about those opportunities, instead of just being fearful of the challenges—will help assure the success of your innovation efforts.

9. Ability to deal with uncertainty.

Innovation projects are by nature uncertain. Innovation leaders and intrapreneurs accept the high level of uncertainty with regard to market, technology, and organizational issues, and are comfortable making decisions based on what they know right now. They also have the flexibility to reverse these decisions should new and relevant information arise, and they often foresee this by having B and C options for their chosen A decision.

By looking for these nine characteristics when identifying innovation leaders and intrapreneurs, you will greatly improve your chances of finding the right people.

Where to Look

Now that you know what you're looking for, what processes can you use to identify the people you need? A few possibilities—from the simple to the more complex—include the following:

- Look around you.

   One simple way to find the people you need is to look for people who persistently follow up on ideas. Scores of employees submit ideas and expect others to deliver. But if you can find one person who keeps showing passion and persistence about her one idea, you'll be farther ahead than if you have 600 people who each submitted an idea but who don't really have an interest in doing the hard work required to make their idea real. With one persistent and qualified contributor—and a good idea—things can happen fast.

   Look for people who are persistent about their ideas, people who work on their ideas independently, and who perhaps even gather other people to help work on their ideas. If the idea is good and you have this kind of person to drive it, you have something to build on.
- Hold an internal business plan competition.

   A much more formalized way to identify potential intrapreneurs is through internal business plan competitions, similar to those held by leading universities. Such competitions are good vehicles for identifying strong ideas as well as the people to drive them forward. Chapter 17, Corporate Business Competition, provides in-depth information on how to conduct such a competition, which companies use to create pools of people with specific skills and an intrapreneurial mindset.

   A well-designed competition accomplishes many things. It helps you identify intrapreneurs, moves forward ideas with real potential, helps participants upgrade their intrapreneurial skills, and provides a method for matching A-grade people with good ideas. With regard to open innovation, an internal competition is a good training exercise to undertake before you move to open innovation. It can help your organization build skills in making innovation happen across silos, skills that will come in handy when you reach out to the world and need to make innovation happen across two or more organizations.

- Start an intrapreneur-in-residence program.

    Why not adopt the entrepreneur-in-residence (EIR) practice that venture capital firms use? The role of an EIR varies, but typically it involves an individual who wants to start a company. Sometimes the entrepreneur has already spent a great deal of time on an idea that the venture company might invest in upon further development, or the EIR acts as a "partner" and helps the venture capitalist evaluate potential deals where the entrepreneur has a particular expertise. An EIR might also spend time with an existing portfolio company to provide his or her functional expertise. In this scenario, the EIR will sometimes enter the company as a full-time executive (typically CEO or some C-level role) if the company and the executive feel there is a good fit.

Why not use this model to establish an intrapreneur-in-residence program within your company? This could be an adjunct to a business plan competition. Having identified people with intrapreneurial potential in the competition, you can assign them to the role of intrapreneur-in-residence for a set period of time. The key here is to define what role this individual would have; this should be based on what outcomes you'd like to achieve with such a program.

This approach is especially useful when companies work to develop a new platform of business activities that consists, in the beginning, of many small, early-stage projects. Until you decide on a full-time executive role in one of the projects, the intrapreneur can consult on many projects.

Questions to Ask

Here are questions that will help you uncover whether a specific person has the traits needed to be an intrapreneur:

- Ask candidates for examples of how they have created results as an individual. In this way you will weed out the many people who tend to hide behind a team effort. Go deeper by asking for cases in which the candidate used passion and drive to make things happen. Inquire about how they overcame organizational, technical, and market obstacles. Ask how they make decisions even when they feel they do not have enough information.

- Ask questions in a direct or even provocative way, and watch for behavioral responses. If the candidate becomes defensive and combative, that would suggest they lack the optimistic attitude and openness required to drive innovation. Instead, look for people who reply in a constructive way that persuades you they can successfully deal with adversity and obstacles.

- Marc Andreesen, co-author of Mosaic and co-founder of Netscape, suggests that you can judge someone's curiosity by asking questions that help you determine how up to date people are on developments in their areas of expertise. For example, he recommends asking people about the top ten most interesting things happening in their field. Someone who is curious and passionate about their work will know what's going on and have opinions about where things are headed.[3]

- Watch for signs that reveal the level of customer focus. This is especially important for intrapreneurs, as they need to have a business mindset and think about jobs that users or customers are trying to get done. It is not enough for an intrapreneur to say he focuses on customers. He needs to put this first and convince you that he has this mindset. Some people will try to fake this. If you get this sense, keep asking questions until you can make up your mind whether the person is bluffing.

- The design and innovation consultancy IDEO uses the term, "T-shaped people," to describe people who are more likely to thrive with innovation. T-shaped people have a principal skill that comprises the vertical leg of the T—perhaps they are mechanical engineers or industrial designers. But they should also be so empathetic that they can branch out into other skills, such as go-to-market strategies, and do those as well. They should be able to explore insights from many different perspectives and recognize patterns of behavior that point to jobs that need to get done. You can look out for this by having potential intrapreneurs describe their own T-shape.

Going Out of This World for Innovation

In this interview, Carsten Hallund Slot, the former Director of Corporate Research and Innovation at Arla Foods (www.arlafoods.com), shares his experiences and insights on how radical innovation projects can help transform "the way to do innovation," and change a company's innovation mindset. It is all about having a passion and believing that innovation can make a difference.

There is a great story about Arla Foods and NASA. Can you briefly tell us about it?

Carsten: The project was about stretching abilities and going to the extreme in order to describe the normalities. If you want to develop new braking systems for cars you can be inspired by Formula 1 or airplanes, but where do you go in the food industry? The International Space Station turned out to be a great option.

Just by daring to go there we set up a radical environment that could foster radical solutions and tools. This stretched our mindset and our way of working.

Consider the task of making two new yoghurts; one for your next-door neighbour and one for a real astronaut in space. The difference is huge, and the fact that we dared to set extreme challenges got the very best out of us. That was the key objective of the NASA project.

During the project, we learned that we were very good at incremental innovation and project management. On the other hand, we were poorly organized and poorly prepared for developing and managing radical innovation. Our structures and tools simply did not support radical innovation. This has changed now.

Besides stretching your abilities and changing the mindset, what else has this project meant for Arla Foods?

Carsten: Most importantly, it has opened our eyes to the opportunities in radical innovation and made us aware of the importance of organizing for radical innovation. This is necessary if you want to stay competitive and be a market leader in the food industry.

The project also gave us a platform to rethink the milk model. What happens if milk is not cooled? What if the cooling chain is broken? This helped us create new business opportunities that we are exploring right now. We have also seen a strong effect on our image and identity

(continued)

among our employees as well as our external stakeholders, including the customers.

As a result of the NASA project we created a new-concept lab, Foodturum, which works on radical business development.

You headed the NASA project. What did you learn in this project? And what did this project mean to your career?

Carsten: I learned the difference between incremental and radical innovation. More importantly, I learned when and how to use and balance the two different sets of tools.

My experiences put me in charge of founding and developing Foodturum. Here, I learned how to bring the insights and knowledge from the NASA project into our business development efforts and thus drive us toward radical improvements for our customers and the users of our products. In this perspective, I have learned a lot on how to lead and manage intrapreneurship in a large and international organization.

Can you elaborate on how to lead and manage such efforts?

Carsten: It is much more about leadership than management, about leading rather than controlling. This is also why I am working hard to implement what I call vision-driven innovation at Arla Foods.

Some key issues include the challenge of how to share knowledge and how to bring different people with different references to work together. We also learned how important it is to anchor radical innovation within our top management. If you are unable to anchor radical innovation initiatives at the top management level and secure their full ownership and support, you cannot be successful with radical innovation.

Why do you think Danish companies excel at innovation and intrapreneurship?

Carsten: We have flat organizational structures with less hierarchy than is common in some other countries. This develops and promotes knowledge-sharing and team work. More importantly, we dare to challenge our mental models and mindsets by going head on with authorities in a constructive manner. We also believe that all people are important and equal, and this makes us capable of excelling with innovation and intrapreneurship in our companies.

Talking about innovation issues, what keeps you awake at night?

Carsten: Passion—I am driven by my passion and belief that innovation can make a huge difference in our daily lives.

Following the success with Foodturum, Carsten became the Director of Corporate Research and Innovation at Arla Foods. This is a direct result of Arla Foods' effort to increase the level of innovation as a part of the overall business growth strategy.

Meet Michael and Johnnie. Profession—Intrapreneurs

In this interview, Michael Kjaer and Johnnie Rask Jensen share their experiences as intrapreneurs and provide you with their take on what it takes to be an intrapreneur.

What is your background and what do you do today that qualifies you to be called an intrapreneur?

Michael: I was the CEO for Crystal Fibre A/S 2000–2008. It is an optical component company based on a cutting-edge technology. The company is owned by NKT, a large industrial conglomerate. I helped build the company from the beginning to become world leader in its field. When I stopped in 2008, the company had 32 employees, annual sales of more than $5 million USD, and a very promising pipeline of commercial opportunities going forward.

I have both a Master of Science and a Business Administration degree. In my past job I worked for Lucent Technologies as product manager and later as sales director in the Optical Fiber Division.

Johnnie: I have worked my entire professional life in the Danfoss Group within product development, marketing, and sales. I have inter-national experience as I helped start a new venture for Danfoss in the UnitedStates, a sales company that combines products from

(continued)

four Danfoss divisions and some non-Danfoss products. We managed to grow business from virtually nothing to $10 million USD in just three years.

Since 2004, I have had the opportunity to head up Danfoss Solutions, a real venture within Danfoss. We are an energy-service company with the mission to deliver bottom-line impact to clients through guaranteed utility cost savings.

I guess that what qualifies me is my track record of being able to make things grow, see opportunities where others see problems, and then to organize and get the masses to move. Furthermore, I know hundreds of Danfoss people at all levels, which helps me tremendously when applying for funding, support, or anything else.

As Michael does, I also have a mix of engineering and business administration education.

Why have you chosen to become intrapreneurs?

Johnnie: I have always dreamed of becoming self-employed, and still do, but I guess that after 20 successful years within Danfoss, it is becoming harder and harder to break loose. When Danfoss approached me for my present position, I thought that this would be a perfect mix between my own ambitions and desires and Danfoss's goals.

Michael: The excitement and the challenge of taking a new technology platform and bringing it to a commercial success has been the biggest driver for me. It also gives me much better learning opportunities than my previous job functions.

Have you had any life-changing experiences on your way to becoming intrapreneurs?

Michael: We always try to celebrate our successes. For me personally getting my first purchase order at Crystal Fibre and getting a license agreement in place for vital Internet protocol (IP) after nine months of negotiations were great experiences.

Which skills and which kind of mindset should an intrapreneur have?

Michael: An intrapreneur must be able to find and bring in the right core team for the business and have good project-management skills to use limited resources efficiently. The ability to understand your customers and correctly gauge customer pain is critical. Political understanding and ability to attract funding from your parent is also beneficial.

Vision, courage, and lots of energy are the most important abilities to possess. You must love what you do and be able to fully accept the risk of failure going into the job. Otherwise you will not have the energy and persistence it takes to be successful.

Johnnie: I think it depends on where you are in a company's life cycle. In the early days, you need vision and drive. Later you must master the talent of organizing. This is a huge transition, and many start-ups don't make it. Above all, I believe you must be a good sales person (internally as well as externally) and have an outstanding robustness to deal with the ups and downs of a venture.

What are the most important things a company should do to develop intrapreneurship?

Johnnie: Allow people to fail. No, encourage people to fail! I strongly believe that, beyond the obvious intrapreneurs, you can find 10 times as many wannabes (especially in Denmark). They just need a little push or encouragement to do it. Companies should also create career paths for intrapreneurs.

What is the best about being an intrapreneur compared to an entrepreneur?

Michael: As an intrapreneur you are able to leverage the strength of the parent company. You can bring in know-how, people, IP, legal expertise. Your parent might provide you with a distribution channel or be a customer of your product. Typically your parent is a much more patient investor than a venture capital-backed startup is. This is especially important for cutting edge and platform-technology based companies like Crystal Fibre, where the road to success is very long.

In short, you are born with a very strong business partner and that greatly increases your chances of success.

Have you ever considered starting your own company?

Michael: Yes, but so far I have not come across the right opportunity.

Johnnie: I have had (and still have) many ideas for companies, but I have been successful at what I have been doing so far, so I have had less of a desire to run my own business.

⚷ᴅ Key Chapter Takeaways

- When it comes to making innovation of all types happen, people matter more than ideas.
- Companies need two different types of people for innovation initiatives:
  1. Innovation leaders who work on the strategic and tactical level to build the internal platform required to develop organizational innovation capabilities.
  2. Intrapreneurs who work on the operational level to turn ideas and research into real products and services that move the business forward.
- When identifying people who will be outstanding innovation leaders and intrapreneurs, look for optimists who have passion and drive, and who are curious and believe in change. Also look for people who have a talent for networking, strong communication skills, and an ability to deal with uncertainty. For innovation leaders, also look for people who see the big picture.
- To find such people, ask prospects questions that will reveal:
  - How up-to-date they are on their professional field.
  - How they've overcome obstacles to make things happen.
  - Whether they are open or defensive and combative.
  - How customer-oriented their thinking is.
  - If they are capable of building on their basic skills so their perspective of innovation will be broadly based.

CHAPTER 6

The Networked Innovation Culture

One must-have component of a strong innovation culture is a strong networking culture. To thrive in an innovation environment that becomes increasingly open and externally oriented, people throughout your organization need to be capable of building and sustaining relationships both internally and externally.

Unfortunately, this is a neglected area of attention for executives as well as for innovation leaders. I remember talking with an executive at a large company after having met with many of the innovation people from his organization. I asked him about his intentions with regard to creating a better networking culture. He did not have any plans. We discussed the benefits of organizational networking analysis that could help identify the people holding important knowledge, as well as the people who were bottlenecks. He saw the relevance. We talked about the importance of being good at relationships in the move toward open innovation. He agreed.

However, when I asked what he would do about the networking culture, I got the same answer. He would do nothing. Why not? "Things like that will take care of themselves," he said.

He could not be more wrong. An innovation culture does not create itself, and the same goes for a networking culture. This requires a top-down approach in which the executives and innovation leaders craft a strategy, set the goals, and provide the means and tools for networking initiatives. In addition, they find ways to get their own skin in the game and thus convince their employees that they are serious.

Why a Networking Culture Is Important

The impetus for creating a networking culture is obvious once you look at the current and future direction of innovation. Let's start by disposing of the myth of the lone genius—the Thomas Edisons and the Alexander Graham Bells of yesteryear—arriving at a break-through innovation on his/her own. This model wasn't true then, and even if it were, it simply does not hold true in today's complex business organizations. Technology and the challenges that must be solved have become so complex that many—perhaps even most—companies can no longer rely solely on their own internal innovation geniuses, no matter how brilliant those people may be.

Innovation is increasingly about having groups of people come together to leverage their diverse talents and expertise to solve multi-faceted challenges that cross multiple disciplines. To make this happen within your organization—and beyond as you move toward open innovation—requires a networking culture that is designed, sup-ported, and modeled by your company's leaders.

Even organizations that are not ready to fully embrace open innovation are finding that employees' mindsets about networking must be stretched as more companies deploy internal R&D func-tions outside the corporate headquarters and around the world. Employees start to wonder who should do innovation and where it should take place. Although this is positive, success in such situations depends heavily on the ability of the employees to initiate, solidify, and leverage external relationships.

Another key motivation for setting up networking initiatives is based on the simple fact that the knowledge of any company is inside the heads of the employees. Discovering and distributing this knowl-edge has always been a challenge, and now, more than ever, the ability to leverage a company's collective knowledge and experience through virtual and face-to-face networks and communities is critical to inno-vation. Furthermore, establishing the ability to bring knowledge and potential new innovation insights in from external sources demands a strong networking culture supported and modeled from the top.

What a Networking Culture Looks Like

So what does a good networking culture looks like? It's such a new concept that there aren't a lot of examples available to illustrate it, but here are some key components of a good networking culture:

- Top executives and innovation leaders have outlined clear strategic reasons why employees need to develop and nurture internal and external relationships. This includes making clear how your company's networking culture links with and supports your innovation strategy (which, of course, is an outgrowth of your overall corporate strategy).
- Among the things to consider when developing your networking culture strategy is what types of networks you hope to build to support your innovation efforts. If your organization is moving toward open innovation, possibilities would include peer-to-peer networks for people working with open innovation in different companies, value- and supply-chain networks, feeder networks, and events and forums connecting problem solvers and innovators with your company.
- Leaders show a genuine and highly visible commitment to networking.
- Leaders must walk the walk, not just talk the talk. By making themselves available at networking events and by being visible users of virtual networking tools, they model the desired behavior and motivate others to participate. After all, who doesn't want a chance to exchange ideas with the top brass?
- Leaders should also share examples of their networking experiences whenever possible. Spread the word about your own and others' networking successes. Hearing leaders talk repeatedly about how networking is helping the organization in its innovation efforts will reinforce the message that this is important.
- Networking initiatives mesh closely with your corporate culture. This is not one-size-fits-all; each company's networking efforts will differ. You can take bits and pieces, concepts and theories, knowledge and experience from others, but you still need to make it work for your own company.
- People are given time and means to network. Frequent opportunities are provided to help individuals polish their personal networking skills. Not everyone is a natural networker. But almost everyone can become good at it with proper training and encouragement.
- Both virtual and face-to-face networking are encouraged and supported. Web 2.0 tools and facilitated networking events maximize the opportunities people have to initiative and build strong relationships.

Three Types of Networkers

As you determine how to build a networking culture within your organization, it's important to understand how networking actually works. One of the most knowledgeable people on organizational networking—and how this supports innovation—is Rob Cross, an associate professor in the management department of the University of Virginia's McIntire School of Commerce. He is also one of the founders of The Network Roundtable. I have learned a lot from my visits and interactions with Rob, and I recommend that you take a look at his web site on www.robcross.org.

Rob Cross has identified three networking types that you should pay attention to within your organization. They are:

- Central connectors.
- Brokers.
- Peripheral people.

Central connectors are those people with the highest number of direct connections. They can be formal leaders—or political players trying to be leaders—whom everyone seeks out either because they make things happen or because they have made themselves bottlenecks. The latter can become a major issue with regard to innovation, where you often need a dynamic flow. Experts are also a type of central connectors who are sometimes overused as everyone goes to them with questions. Sometimes experts must be protected.

Brokers are high-leverage employees who connect people across boundaries, such as functions, skills, geography, hierarchy, ethnicity, and gender. These people have the leverage ability to drive change, diffusion, or innovation, and they can also act in key liaison or cross-process roles.

According to Cross, brokers often sit in tipping-point positions and, therefore, diffuse information faster than leaders and central connectors. Even in a small group, brokers are the most effective means to diffuse information. Brokers have ground-level credibility and acknowledged expertise in the eyes of their peers. They are much more likely to be sought out and listened to than a designated expert or leader who may not be influential in the network. Brokers bridge diverse perspectives and understand cultural norms and practices of different groups in ways that those familiar and comfortable within their own group often cannot.

Peripheral people could be new people, experts, sales people, poor performers, or cultural misfits. They sit on the edge of the network, and

Cross has learned that typically 30 to 40 percent of peripheral people would like to get better connected but have run into obstacles. They are a resource of untapped expertise but are substantial flight risks. Peripheral people are particularly in need of education about how to network; they will also need more encouragement than others to participate in networking.

Knowing these different types should prompt you to ask questions about what networking types you have within your organization and what type of networking approaches might work best. For example, if your company has a lot of peripheral people, you'll need to devote more time to training in networking skills. Also, as a leader, think about how you can work best with the different types to be able to get the most out of them.

Virtual Tools

Many people view networking as a nice-to-do as opposed to a must-do task, and the day-to-day pressures of business often cause networking to fall to the bottom of the to-do list. So you can't just assume networking will happen on its own. You must build mechanisms into your workplace that encourage people to network regularly, both internally and externally. And as mentioned earlier, you will want to use a variety of both virtual networking tools and live networking opportunities.

Let's talk about virtual tools first. Web 2.0 applications are making it possible for companies of all sizes to enable employees at all levels to participate in activities that help them build and nurture stronger networks of contacts across the organization. These tools, which are quick, easy, and inexpensive, include:

- Blogs.
- Information tagging.
- Microblogging (think Twitter).
- Social networks.
- Wikis.
- Podcasts.

Companies have reported benefits from enabling employees to interact on closed company networks, using text-message-like technology in which users are limited to very few words on each post. The benefits include making it easier for employees to stay connected with each other, improving the flow of relevant information across departments, and building bridges across gaps between worldwide locations.[2] Even with Twitter's 140-character limit, people can learn more about each other personally and professionally, leading to stronger ties and greater willingness to exchange information and collaborate.

The consulting firm of McKinsey & Company has been tracking the growing adoption of these technologies within corporations for several years. Their study of companies that have used Web 2.0 technologies internally has revealed that just providing these tools is not enough. You can't just build it and expect people to jump right in and participate. Companies must do the hard work involved in ensuring the widespread participation that will make these tools a success.

To maximize your chances for success with these tools, McKinsey recommends:[3]

- Providing visible support from leaders.
- Allowing employees to determine the best use for a virtual tool instead of dictating how it should be used.
- Providing highly visible recognition to people who use the tools in outstanding ways.
- Finding ways to reduce the fears leaders and managers can have about how these tools will be used. These tools can bring dissent within an organization to the surface. It's a wise policy to ban anonymous postings on a blog or social network and to have an auditing function in place to identify inappropriate postings.

Web Tools in Action

Web 2.0 applications can greatly improve the flow of knowledge within an organization, including information related to innovation. Here's an example:

A global company that I have been involved with wanted to overcome bottlenecks in their innovation process. It had a lot of ideas coming in from all parts of the organization, but it didn't have a way to prioritize the ideas and to allocate them to people who could act on them. Through an external service provider, the company used Web

2.0 technology to run idea exchanges across different departments. It was able to generate ideas, screen them, and create a shortlist of the most important ideas.

An equally important outcome was that people throughout the organization were able to work together on ideas and to exchange information easily. This led to stronger relationships and continued information sharing after the idea exchanges were completed.

Face-to-Face Networking

A few years back, I helped a fairly large company at the intersection of innovation and networks/relationships. What we learned from our work provides some important guidance about how to organize face-to-face networking opportunities.

This project touched on issues such as:

- Creating an informal platform where employees could share ideas and build on them together.
- Helping employees understand the value of relationships and developing tools that could help grow their networking skills.
- Increasing the strength of internal relationships between employees and then developing stronger external ties.

We held several short informal sessions in which we discussed how innovation and entrepreneurship could flourish even more. Rather than PowerPoint presentations, the sessions were like speaker interviews and discussion groups. Through this work I arrived at five things to consider when you want to create an internal idea marketplace.

1. **Short length, high frequency:** Hold short, frequent sessions on relevant topics. Time is critical in business today, and you must give your people as many chances to connect with each other while spending as little time as possible. Consider lunch-and-learn sessions; everyone has to eat, so why not do it while you interact with others?
2. **Turn sessions into idea platforms:** There is no shortage of people with ideas. But there is a shortage of people who

excel at bringing ideas out of their own minds. You could turn these sessions into a platform—a tool for receiving, sharing, and developing ideas. Such platforms are missing in many companies. To make these platforms as effective as possible:

- Use boards—physical as well as virtual—on which employees can briefly explain their ideas and get in touch with each other.
- Use facilitators (well-connected employees) who can help less-connected colleagues get in touch with each other.
- Use elevator pitches. Give employees three minutes to explain their idea and their needs. The response from their peers will provide a strong indicator about whether to move forward with the ideas.

Many companies say they have platforms for receiving ideas. Sometimes the platform is just a mailbox. That is okay as long as you avoid the worst mistake—no follow-up and no ongoing communication with those who submit ideas.

3. Help managers see the bigger picture: Managers will have two main concerns about internal idea marketplaces. How do we control how much time employees spend, and how do we know it is worthwhile? How will idea platforms affect our current project portfolio? Fair enough, but in reality these are often not that problematic. People working on projects in which they are driven by passion will find the time to work on it. Their day jobs will not suffer much, making it easier for managers to cut a bit of slack in such cases.

An idea-generation project should be monitored and managed to make sure it fits into the overall portfolio strategy. Keep the reporting mechanism as loose as possible. Managers should focus not only on ideas but also on identifying the people who can drive opportunities forward. If you create a forum where people can speak freely, you will find innovators you didn't know you had.

4. Make decisions faster: Of course, employees should use the marketplace to exchange feedback. But you could also develop a decision-making tool for the ideas. Let's call this a Pitch Pit. Imagine an open session in which teams present

their ideas to senior managers who have the authority to make go/no-go decisions on the spot.

A "go" decision should result in the necessary resources (time to work on the idea, access to other parts of the organization, and financial support) to determine whether the project is worthwhile. If a "no-go" decision is made, the idea should be killed effectively—or merged with other promising ideas. This is a great opportunity for letting marketplace facilitators build their overview and networking skills.

5. Blend the virtual and the real by using wiki-style project sites: Wiki-style project sites could be established for knowledge sharing, co-creation, and learning purposes. Such sites could also include a vote-of-trust mechanism enabling everyone to see how much the organization believes in the specific idea. The transparency and collaboration in these sites will help senior managers prepare for their appearance in the Pitch Pit.

In an innovation marketplace, projects will be formed across organizational silos, and by working on real—although early stage—projects, employees really get to know each other. Such relationships will be valuable, even though many projects will fail. By the way, imagine what can be done if you involve external partners in such activities. Yes, there will be difficulties in handling this, but the rewards can be worth it.

Potential Roadblocks

In working with companies that are trying to build a networking culture, here are some reasons I've identified for why such efforts can fail or not reach the hoped-for degree of success:

- Lack of time and skills: Many of us simply do not have the time or skills to network and build relationships. It is necessary to develop a strategy and initiate projects, but the executives and you, as an innovation leader, also need to give your people time to acquire networking skills and the time to invest in initiating and maintaining both internal and external relationships.

- Lack of focus: A community or a network will only work if it connects people who share a common experience, passion, interest, affiliation, or goal. Your people need to have ways to find and join groups that are right for them and right for your company. In other words, you and those you lead should only network when there is a good reason to do so. Random networking rarely results in anything but wasted time, which devalues networking in people's minds and makes it harder to encourage them to try it again.

- We are too old: Many people over 28 years old just don't see the value of Web 2.0 networking tools such as Facebook, LinkedIn, and Twitter. We have a real generation gap here. We, the older and wiser ones, are still in charge, but this will begin to change in five years' time as we get the first leaders from the Facebook generation. Ten years on, they will define the rules. Why not try to figure out how it works now instead of waiting?

    Some organizations are already headed down this path. For example, Best Buy's retail employees are mostly 16- to 24-year-olds. Recently, six young, tech-savvy workers joined with three professional developers to build online collaboration into Best Buy's operations. The team quickly and cheaply created a wiki that lets the company's employees contribute insights on competition and popular trends, all good grist for innovation efforts.

    There is evidence that older generations are adapting to a Web 2.0 world and doing so very rapidly. For example, in July 2009, Facebook's user demographics showed that the largest block of users, 28.2 percent overall, were in the 35–54-age group. During the previous six months, users aged 55 and over had grown from just 950,000 to 5.9 million.[4] Personally, I've found LinkedIn to be tremendously efficient for building a global virtual network of people who are interested in the issues I deal with in my work. I've been able to connect with hundreds of people who have shared their insights into the challenges of leading innovation. LinkedIn can also be used to build a group that includes only people within your company, so it's a quick, effective tool for encouraging networking on innovation issues across your organization.

- Lack of commitment and structure

    The networking-will-take-care-of-itself-and-you-do-not-need-to-work-at-it attitude is not the approach to take toward building what increasingly is a core innovation skill. Building a networking culture requires commitment and structure to support it.

In studying networks across many organizations, Rob Cross and his colleagues have identified three other common problems[5] that impede networking and collaboration in organizations both large and small:

1. No communication: Does the structure of your company keep apart people who might team up for innovation? The problem could be related to logistics, geography, or bureaucracy. Identify the causes of such impediments, and put in place systems to help people work around them. Eliminate silos, and encourage cross-functional networking and collaboration.
2. Bad gatekeepers: Do a handful of experts dominate your company's information and decision-making networks? Are these gatekeepers good judges of new ideas, or does their expertise in one area blind them to the potential of new ideas from other areas? Set up wikis and similar tools to encourage information sharing to make sure no one person or one group has a stranglehold on information.
3. Insularity: If you've outsourced innovation to reduce development time and costs, have you built a strong network with formal lines of communications to make sure you're always on top of what's happening with your external partner? Don't rely on just informal connections between key employees at the companies; this can lead to frustration and unpleasant surprises. It becomes equally important to avoid insularity as you move toward open innovation. Having systems in place that encourage people to build strong relationships with external partners is essential in an open innovation environment.

⚿ Key Chapter Takeaways

- A networking culture is a critical part of an innovation culture that aspires to become more and more open and external-oriented. Your company needs to have strategies in place to build networking expertise within your organization.
- Even if you're not using an open innovation model, employees who are operating in a global community need to know how to network with people in far-flung locations.
- A networking culture has:
  - A clear statement of strategic reasons people need to develop and nurture internal and external relationships.
  - Leadership commitment to networking.
  - Networking initiatives that mesh closely with your corporate culture.
  - Frequent virtual and face-to-face opportunities for people to polish their personal networking skills.
- Pay close attention to the three types of networkers in your organization: central connectors, brokers, and peripheral people.
- Deploy Web 2.0 applications to facilitate networking internally and externally.
- To maximize the effectiveness of face-to-face networking:
  - Emphasize short length, high frequency.
  - Turn sessions into idea platforms.
  - Help managers keep their eye on the big picture so they don't cause roadblocks because they worry that their employees who are networking are taking time away from their real work.
  - Make quick decisions on ideas contributed to idea marketplaces.
  - Use wiki-style project sites to blend the real and the virtual.
- Avoid these roadblocks to a building a networking culture:
  - Not enough time or skills.
  - Lack of focus, commitment, structure, and communication.
  - Bad gatekeepers.
  - Insularity.

PART

II

ROADBLOCKS

All forms of innovation, including open innovation, are fraught with peril. Many of the roadblocks you will encounter have to do with people-related issues. Unfortunately, at too many companies when these problems arise, the response is to assume there is something wrong with the process being used. So the old process is thrown out and yet another new process is brought in without the underlying problem ever being solved. This creates a process-of-the-month environment, in which people get very jaded about being told to try yet another new way to tackle innovation.

In this section, we focus on the people side as we discuss how senior executives and what I call corporate antibodies can get in the way of innovation. I'll also provide some ideas on proactive ways to work around these roadblocks. The last chapter in this part deals with radical innovation, and I am quite it will be provocative to some of you.

7

Why Top Executives Do Not Get Innovation, Much Less Open Innovation—and What to Do About It

Many innovation leaders struggle to get the support they need from executives higher up in the organization. Top executives can be skilled at talking the talk about innovation, especially in public venues, but frequently fail to walk the walk when it comes to making key choices that determine whether an innovation project will happen or die on the vine.

This may seem paradoxical, because everyone knows that innovation, and increasingly open innovation, is what drives business success in the twenty-first century, right? Well, sort of. Although corporate leaders may intellectually accept the need for innovation and tout their commitment to innovation at every opportunity, they often fail to really understand innovation. As a result, they become a major roadblock in your path to succeed as innovation leader.

In 2007, the Center for Creative Leadership sought to identify leadership trends by surveying 247 senior executives and leaders who, among them, had more than 15 years of management experience and managed more than 500 people. Fifty percent of these leaders believed their organization was top in class in innovation.[1] Either they do not want to admit otherwise, or their standard for top of class (which is usually defined as the top 5 to 10 percent) is very low. My estimate, based on experience with organizations around the world, is that less than 10 percent of companies are world-class innovators.

Yet even if we accept the 50 percent figure as being accurate, that still leaves plenty of room for improvement. So wouldn't you assume that these leaders would pursue every possible avenue to improve their organization's innovation capabilities? Unfortunately, the responses to the next question show that's not the case. When asked what they were doing to promote innovation in their organizations, the percentages of respondents who said their companies were trying various strategies were surprisingly low.

For example, the most popular strategy, adopting overt innovation processes, was named by only 25 percent of respondents as something their company was doing. Only 17 percent said they focus on talent/talent development, the second most often-used category. And just 13 percent said they had rewards/recognition programs to support innovation.

I contend that these responses show that CEOs are actually doing surprisingly little to build innovation cultures in their companies. If they were, surely more than 10 percent of these leaders would say they were following best practices in their industry in their pursuit of innovation.[2] Perhaps this is why only about 25 percent of the members of my network groups say their CEO has the right mindset and understanding of innovation to support the company's innovation success.

The Whys

Here are some reasons why I believe CEOs and other C-level officers often don't support innovation, even though the business climate of our time demands that innovation, including the open variety, be a core capability:

- The demand for short-term gains nearly always wins the day.

    Top executives at public companies are under enormous pressure to produce strong financial results each and every quarter. This is the area in which they are rewarded for producing results, and their job security increasingly depends on it, as shown by an annual study conducted by Booz Allen from 1995 to 2006. In tracking CEO turnover rates at the world's 2,500 largest publicly traded companies, Booz Allen found that annual CEO turnover grew by 50 percent during that period, meaning CEOs are in greater peril overall. Equally interesting, a CEO who delivered below-average investor returns stayed in office as long as high performers in 1995, but by 2006, a CEO who delivered above-average returns was almost twice as likely as one delivering subpar returns to remain CEO for more than seven years.[3]

There simply is no room in this equation for CEOs to put their necks on the line and support investments in innovation efforts that won't produce near-term results or those that may even have a negative impact on the bottom line for some period of time. Thus we find ourselves in a world in which companies put too much focus on incremental innovation. In an ideal world, boards would demand that investments in innovation be made on a widely accepted norm of 80 percent incremental and 20 percent radical to assure the long-term health of the organization. But few organizations have metrics for measuring innovation, and boards don't pay executives based on innovation objectives. Dynamic values such as entrepreneurship, creativity, and risk-taking are not measured, let alone valued at bonus time. This leads to an overemphasis on incremental innovation.

Current leaders got to the top of the heap by being able to produce on the static financial metrics that are so beloved on Wall Street. Often, it is only when a crisis strikes and a company is in deep trouble—and not meeting those financial metrics—that many boards start demanding innovation, which, of course, can't be cranked up overnight.

Having worked with several large companies still controlled by their founders, I would say the exceptions to this tend to be such companies. They are less susceptible to this problem because founders are generally deeply committed to assuring their company's long-term health, not just making the quarterly numbers.

- They missed out on innovation education.

Many of today's top executives got their business education before innovation was a significant part of the curriculum at many MBA programs. They could compensate for this with experience, but many also missed being trained on the job, because innovation training usually goes down through organizations, not upward. And when they gained most of their experience, innovation was even more underserved than today. They were trained to be problem solvers, not innovators.

In the early to mid-1990s, a major breakthrough on innovation education happened when thought leaders such as Clayton Christensen, Gary Hamel, C. K. Prahalad, and others started to drive attention to innovation. That's when the top business schools began to give innovation a higher priority in their MBA programs. The people educated in these programs are now reaching the top executive level. I hope this will give us leaders who better understand how to develop an innovation strategy and stick to it—in good as well as in bad times.

A positive sign of change is that innovation leaders who transfer to new companies have begun reaching the top executive level. I know of several innovation leaders who have advanced to the top level when they transferred to companies in need of an innovation strategy. They started as innovation leaders, but they were quickly promoted when the CEO of the new company realized the potential of their mindset and skills.

- Top executives are risk-averse.

  Innovation, especially open innovation, is scary on many levels. People who reached the top of their organization because of their knowledge of the existing business aren't that interested in considering a new business model or going after an amazing, yet high-risk breakthrough innovation when that may mean their expertise in the business might become obsolete. And who wants to risk having a major innovation effort fail on their watch?

  People who truly understand innovation embrace failure as an inherent part of innovation. They realize that often big lessons that lead to success come from the biggest failures. An attitude that doesn't allow for failure is contrary to an innovation culture, yet that's the kind of attitude that too many company leaders possess.

- Top executives are control freaks.

  Innovation done well requires the right people as well as the right processes. If there are no processes in place, this can lead to confusion and the feeling of having no control of things. And although many top executives should be trained to set up processes, they still need to make room for the unexpected and create an environment where they can deal with many uncertainties. You have to let go of some control, which can be a difficult thing for top executives who want to run a tight ship. Especially in an open innovation environment, being able to let go of some control so that you can create a win/win situation for your external partners becomes important.

- Leaders may lack the X-vision.

    Leaders and managers are often promoted because they excel within just one business function, such as R&D, sales, supply chain, or finance. They have difficulties seeing across functions and combining several elements within a value chain and innovation process. They lack the X-vision—the ability to work across business functions and with many types of innovation to turn ideas into profitable products, services, or business methods—and they do not train their employees to have X-vision skills, either. X-vision is very much about mindset, and can be developed through training and coaching, as well as through job rotation programs.

- They lack the understanding of why a networking culture is important for open innovation.

    As I discussed in Chapter 6, in a world of open innovation you need to be an expert at networking and building relationships. This holds true at the corporate level as well as the personal level. So I ask leaders and managers where their strategy, commitment, and the structure needed to create a networking culture is. Many of them have not bothered to give this important subject any thought.

    As open innovation grows, these executives will hear of many cases that showcase why a networking culture is important. This exposure will help them understand the importance of cultivating a networking culture. Then they can initiate more operationally minded initiatives. I know of a vice president at a global company who is experimenting on this. The VP has identified five people from their innovation unit who already have some external contacts within different fields. They have been given a budget and the very open-ended goal to spend the year establishing relationships that could lead to new kinds of innovation. They will learn as they go and adjust goals and budgets along the way.

- Top executives are too far away from the action.

It is easy to preach innovation when you do not have to make it happen. I have been in several situations in which innovation leaders have to struggle with middle managers who prefer to focus on their day-to-day business, rather than support innovation efforts that might take away resources here and now, but that will contribute significantly to the overall business in the future.

The problem is that top executives reward middle managers for getting stuff done and executing flawlessly. This can be counter-intuitive to innovating. But top executives are often too far away from the action to understand how this compensation structure makes it harder for innovation leaders to succeed on their stated goals. This is why, when you really need the support of the CEO in a fight for resources or in a battle of wills with another executive, you'll often find that your CEO sides with the status quo. Most leaders are more wedded to rewarding the core business rather than pursuing something new and untested.

Unfortunately, board members tend to have the same problem and thus are not effective at driving C-level executives toward innovation. In the name of good corporate governance, over the last few decades insiders who were intimately familiar with a company have been increasingly replaced by outside board members. These people are often selected based on their star power and name recognition, and are not really connected with the company. As such they may not have much understanding of the complex technologies at the core of the organization. The outside board members may be able to talk a good game to Wall Street, but when it comes to how to set policy for the organization, they often do not have the insight to foster innovation.

How to Operate in This Environment

It is a major challenge for an innovation leader to operate in an environment in which the top executives don't get innovation or—perhaps even worse—do understand it but are unwilling to fully embrace it because it means going against the board of directors' focus on short-term financial goals. What can you do to thrive in such an environment, especially if you're trying to build something as complex as open innovation capabilities? Based on my experiences, here are some methods to apply:

- Challenge and stretch the mindsets of the top executives

  Innovation is a holistic activity that needs to be understood and embraced by everyone from the top to the bottom. For this reason, your innovation training initiatives should include top executives. In addition to building their knowledge of how innovation actually works, this will also help create a common language around innovation, one of the factors that is important for helping innovation work.

  I once did a presentation at a company where my audience was a fairly typical crowd—the R&D guys and a few innovation leaders. But there was one person who was not part of the usual suspects. It was a finance guy who asked good questions and was really engaged. It was not until the end of the presentation that I learned he was not just a finance guy; he was actually the CFO. The innovation leader who had recently joined the company was having success in trying to make all executives understand they had a role to play when it comes to innovation. The innovation leader used the Ten Types of Innovation framework (see Appendix) to make the CFO understand he should also be involved.

  The level of a company's innovation culture and efforts can generally be gauged by the number and type of people who attend internal innovation events. If the event has been publicized to the whole company and all business areas—not just to those who are supposed to care about innovation—you can simply look at the diversity of the participants. The more diverse the attendance—both in terms of business areas and in terms of people from all levels—the better the innovation culture. So when you set up training efforts and work to create the common language, make sure you reach out to everyone, including senior executives.
- Help your top executives understand—and buy into—the idea that the innovation strategy should be tightly linked to the overall strategy.

This will help them commit personally, as they are all vested in the overall strategy. Create a roadmap for the executives, which shows the path from the corporate strategy to the innovation strategy and then through the various elements of innovation you're pursuing. Any time you're doing a presentation, be sure to include this roadmap as a reminder of why you're doing the presentation.

Also in this context, you must understand the power of peer pressure, even at the executive level. Whenever possible, major decisions should be made in a group setting. When leaders commit to providing resources and support in front of their peers, it's easier to hold them accountable if they later try to renege on their commitments.

- Understand what really matters to the top executives and especially to the CEO.

  Is the CEO more focused on the bottom line (streamlining processes, cutting costs, and such) or the top line (growing sales)? Make sure you initiate innovation projects in areas on which top executives are focused, and get support from key people who influence this preference. If you can find ways to get top executives personally committed to innovation efforts because those efforts match what really matters to them, you can make good long-term progress by getting even small wins in those areas. This can help you win the backing needed to move into other, bigger, innovation initiatives later.

- Leverage the power of corporate communications.

  If you have to really educate your top executives on innovation, you should invest heavily in building strong working relationships with your corporate communications department. Make sure they understand what you're doing and its importance to the company. They can help generate stories—both internally and externally—that create a perception that the company is making strides in innovation, while keeping people aware that there is ample room to improve. This perception can help when you need to ask for resources and support.

- Do not start too many initiatives.

  Most innovation leaders are highly driven people who thrive on change and are capable of keeping many balls in the air at the same time. But remember that many leaders do not share these traits; they prefer that things not change and aren't interested in taking on anything new. Thus, while you're tempted to start a flurry of initiatives, it is better to narrow your focus rather than going in many directions at once.

- Get some small wins.

    Achieving some small successes can help convince top executives that you understand the need for the short-term results they value. This will build confidence in your overall program and give you credibility for going after larger innovation goals.

The one part of the system over which you have little influence is the board of directors. Since they choose the CEO and influence top executives through the CEO, as well as decide the basis for salary raises and bonuses, they have a huge impact on whether innovation gets the support it needs. Unfortunately, there is little you can do as an innovation leader to influence the board.

Which brings us to a final word of advice: If you find yourself constantly hitting your head against the wall because of roadblocks thrown up by a leadership team that does not understand or support innovation, you need to ask yourself if you are in the right place. And you probably need to get out. In most situations, I would advise giving yourself a maximum of two years before giving up on being able to help senior executives become true supporters of innovation.

⚷═🗝 Key Chapter Takeaways

- Senior executives are often major roadblocks to innovation because they:
    - Are focused on short-term gains.
    - Missed out on innovation education
    - Are risk-averse.
    - Are control freaks.
    - Lack the X-vision.
    - Don't understand why a networking culture is important.
    - Are too far away from the action when it comes to innovation.

(continued)

- You can overcome these problems by:
  - Challenging and stretching the mindset of top executives.
  - Helping them understand and buy into the creation of a tight link between innovation strategy and the overall corporate strategy.
  - Understanding what really matters to top executives.
  - Leveraging the power of corporate communications.
  - Gaining some small wins and not starting too many innovation initiatives at once.

Defeating the Corporate Antibodies

Change is frightening to many elements inside the typical organization. Change threatens people's power, their status, their egos, and, in some situations, even their jobs. Change can make someone's expertise obsolete and thereby make that person obsolete as well. Because people are afraid of change, innovation efforts often cause the eruption of corporate antibodies that fight to kill innovation and maintain the status quo.

The factors that cause angst within a closed system of innovation may prove to be even more threatening when a company shifts toward open innovation. Executives and managers may feel they can control the degree of change and shape it to their own needs as long as everything is happening within the organization. But start to bring outside forces in, and it's a whole new ballgame. One reason is that change related to open innovation impacts the whole company. It is not just driven from R&D or the innovation guys. If you want to succeed in open innovation, you have to make changes in business functions, such as sales, supply chain, production, and others, to accommodate your new external partners. This can be scary to many people.

Detecting Antibodies

The signs that corporate antibodies are at work can be heard in statements such as:

- "We already tried that and couldn't make it work."
- "What we're doing has worked fine for years; there is no need to change."

- "Our current product is still profitable; I don't see why we need to spend money on something new that might not even work out."
- "We already explored that idea years ago but decided against it."
- "If that were a good idea, we'd already have thought of it. After all, we are the experts on this." (Said about an idea coming from the outside.)
- "Let me just play devil's advocate here . . ."
- "Of course, I support innovation, but I just don't think this is the right time to make a big change. The market isn't ready."

People who are making these types of statements may truly believe that what they're doing is best for the company. Or they may be putting their personal interests ahead of company loyalty. Some people also become antibodies because they don't feel their opinions are given enough weight. Such feelings can cause people to continuously take the negative side or play devil's advocate. The phrase "I hate to bring this up, but . . ." comes from them a lot, followed by a boatload of negativity.

This is not to say that anyone who questions the need for change or the direction that change is taking is an antibody. Sound feedback is needed from many quarters for real innovation to occur. But what I'm talking about is not constructive criticism. Rather it is the relentless negativity, foot dragging, and throwing up of needless roadblocks that pose a true threat to innovation ever becoming a reality.

Here's how the corporate antibodies often play out during the three stages of innovation:

1. Discovery.
   Often in this early phase, people will appear to be sceptics but will generally still be open-minded. Antibodies are often not yet a real problem.
2. Incubation.
   This can be where the big battles occur as people begin to understand how the proposed innovation might put their status or influence at risk. Most will be inclined to see change as a threat, not as an opportunity. So you'll become locked

in power battles as people decide that they want to block you instead of back you.

3. Acceleration.

In this final phase, you'll have to deal with corporate politics at its toughest. When it becomes clear that the innovation is going forward, some people will even fight to own it and control it, even if they fought against the innovation at every step of the way up to this point.

Some Solutions

Recognizing that corporate antibodies are likely to show up at some point in your innovation process and having strategies in place to deal with them should help you derail some of the people who want to impede change and maintain the status quo. Here are some potential solutions:

- Make people backers rather than blockers.

    It's never too early to start this. By being proactive rather than reactive, you can sometimes co-opt the antibodies into the process in a way that satisfies their egos and makes them feel their ideas and authority are being appropriately recognized. The key is to make them feel they can play a valuable role in shaping the company's future, including their own destiny. Bring people together to facilitate knowledge sharing and the building of new relationships that broaden everyone's perspectives. Keep people involved in the innovation process.

- Stay below the radar.

    In some situations, the best choice is to stay below the radar as long as possible. Don't become too interesting too early. This will help you avoid people who want to own the idea or process, or who want to apply standard corporate processes to the project even though this can kill it.

- Have frameworks and processes in place.

    Many internal innovation debacles can partly be avoided by setting internal rules about how to bring innovation projects forward. With a framework and process in place, it becomes easier to move projects forward without having them get hung up in destructive internal warfare. This, however, can be difficult in organizations where the executives do not have a good understanding of how innovation works, as I discussed in Chapter 7. This is one more reason to make sure you educate top leaders about innovation.

- Provide high autonomy.

    Having innovation councils with high autonomy or units with their own assigned budgets and goals are other ways to get around the damage that can be done by corporate antibodies. Such structures help shelter new ideas against situations in which executives are not willing to spend their political capital in supporting innovation or when they believe the change will impact their own career negatively.

Mastering Stakeholder Management

You need to understand that the projects you run affect other people. The more people you affect, the more likely it is that your actions will impact people having the power and influence to make or break your project. This makes stakeholder management a critical discipline for you to master if you want to become successful with your innovation projects.

You can get an idea of stakeholder management by thinking in terms of three steps: identification, profiling, and communication.

1. Identify your stakeholders.

    The first step is to figure out who your stakeholders are. Think of internal and external people who can affect your project in both positive and negative ways, and people who might feel threatened or stand to gain from your project. Think not only of the obvious people, such as your boss, but also of influencers who are not on a formal organization chart. Prioritize and place important stakeholders on a short list.

    As criteria for placing people on the short list, ask yourself two questions: Does this person hold any impact on my project right now? Will this person have a high impact now, soon, or late in the project?

    Although working your stakeholders is important, you will often lack the time to work with all of them, so you need to prioritize them early on. However, you should always be prepared to change the status of the stakeholders and add new stakeholders when you learn of people being affected by your project.

2. Profile your stakeholders.

The next step is to create short profiles of the stakeholders you have placed on your short list. Compile information such as:

- Orientation: Is the stakeholder internal or external?
- General information: What are the name, job function, contact information, and short bio of the stakeholder?
- View: Do you see the stakeholder as an advocate, supporter, neutral, critic, or a blocker of the project? Why?
- Impact: Does the stakeholder have a strong, medium, or weak impact on your project? Why?
- Time: Is the impact now, soon, or late in the project life cycle?
- Type of influence: Does the stakeholder hold a formal/direct or an informal/indirect influence on the project? Why?
- Key interests: What are the key financial or emotional interests of the stakeholder with regard to your project?
- The circle of influence: Who influences the stakeholder generally, and who influences the stakeholder's opinion of you? To which degree are you connected with the stakeholder and his influencers?

3. Communicate with your stakeholders.

The last step is to figure out what you want from your stakeholders and what you can offer them—and then communicate with them.

You might not feel you are ready to do so, but you need to communicate with your stakeholders early and often. This lets them know what you are doing, and you can use their reactions to make changes that can increase the likelihood of success for your project.

People are usually quite open about their views, and the best way to start building successful relationships with your stakeholders is to talk directly with them. If you have problems getting in touch with the stakeholders, you might have to use more informal approaches such as "random meetings" in which you seek out places with a good chance of delivering an elevator pitch that might make the stakeholder more interested in your project.

You should do your homework before these meetings and interactions. Besides having crafted a profile, you should also know the most compelling messages to use with each stakeholder, and you should be able to deliver quick and concise elevator pitches based on these messages.

Later, in Chapter 16, we will look further into how you can improve selling your ideas and visions by using a value proposition and elevator pitches. This is a key skill you need to master as an innovation leader and intrapreneur.

Key Chapter Takeaways

- Because change frightens many people, the prospect of change caused by innovation often causes the eruption of corporate antibodies.
- Corporate antibodies are most likely to arise during the incubation and acceleration phases of innovation.
- You can fight corporate antibodies by:
  - Making people backers rather than blockers.
  - Staying below the radar.
  - Having frameworks and processes in place.
  - Providing high autonomy to your innovation councils.
- Stakeholder management is a key component of fighting off corporate antibodies. You should:
  - Identify and profile all stakeholders.
  - Communicate with your stakeholders.

9

Radical Innovation as a Roadblock

Here's a provocative idea: Radical innovation is too difficult for most companies, and they should play it safer when it comes to innovation.

When I proposed this idea on my blog, it elicited a flurry of responses, many of them expressing dismay at the idea that companies should give up on radical innovation. My objective had been to start a discussion that could lead innovation leaders to think hard about radical innovation and force them to consider to what extent—if at all—they should initiate radical innovation projects.

To begin to understand why some companies opt not to focus on radical innovation, let's first define what we're talking about when we say radical innovation. A commonly accepted definition is that we talk about projects with an identified team and budget that are perceived as having the potential to offer either new-to-the-world performance features, significant (5–10 times) improvement in known features, or significant (30–50 percent) reduction in cost. This definition was developed by the Radical Innovation Group, which also developed the previously mentioned DIA model.

Focusing on radical innovation can be a big roadblock or even a recipe for complete failure when companies are in the early stages of building an innovation mindset, culture, and capacities. Here are five reasons I gave in my blog that most companies should forget about radical innovation:

1. It will typically take five to seven years before you see results on radical innovation projects.

    With such a timeline, it's not unusual for projects to never even get finished. You start a project when times have been good enough long enough (at least a couple of years) that you dare to invest. Then you hesitate as good times come to an end, and you shut it down when we hit a crisis, like now. This gives you no results despite heavy investments, and you have to deal with frustrated employees who may have devoted literally years of their work lives to something that never really got off the ground.

    Rightly or wrongly, many top executives have decided that innovation is expendable during a business downturn. As a result, over the past several recessions so much has been cut from most companies' R&D programs that it is questionable whether many organizations actually have the capabilities needed to successfully pursue radical innovation. By the time these capabilities are built back up, the next recession may be upon us. This is why it's not a surprise that much of the innovation that does come out of a recession—and it is often a considerable amount—comes from startups and not from big companies.

2. Few executives, leaders, managers, and employees have successful experiences with radical innovation.

    As this is still such a new discipline, companies simply lack the skills, mindset, and knowledge needed to successfully complete radical innovation projects. The projects get too little time to show results, and they become obvious targets for cost cutting by executives and leaders lacking the know-how and the patience to make radical innovation successful.

3. Innovation projects that are closer to incremental rather than radical innovation are more likely to succeed, making such projects more acceptable to risk-averse executives and managers.

    I even suspect such projects could give a better return on investment than radical innovation projects, although I admit I have not found data to prove this.

4. Companies can simply buy startups with radical projects under way and integrate them into their core business, using their well-established brand and sales channels.

   This could be a dangerous approach because companies tend to make such projects fit their organization rather than fit the needs of the customers. Also, fewer than 50 percent of mergers and acquisitions actually deliver the intended results. The chances of success increase when you develop entirely new platforms based on the radical innovation projects you have acquired and let them live their own lives.

5. It is not only difficult for big companies to create radical innovations, it is often contrary to their best interest and culture.

   As the current market leaders, big companies have no incentive to change. They want to keep the status quo, and this mindset can blind them to the fact that other organizations—usually smaller, nimbler ones—will make sure the disruption comes. They prefer to play it safe rather than setting out for the tough job of cannibalizing and reinventing themselves.

Choosing This Path

Of course, as many of those who responded to my blog on this topic noted, some companies have been successful with radical innovation projects. Apple is one such company that was mentioned often. The iPod and the iPhone were both game changers. When radical innovation is done successfully, companies can dominate industries and earn huge payoffs. In the earlier interview with Mads Prebensen from Grundfos New Business Development, we also learned that you can benefit a lot from having a platform for radical innovation where new projects can be given futures out of the core and with structures that fit their needs.

In the long run, a portfolio approach to innovation probably works best for most companies, provided the right innovation culture and support systems are in place. The portfolio approach involves pursuing some incremental projects, some breakthrough projects (defined as meaningful change that gives consumers something demonstrably new), and some radical innovation projects, with a higher percentage of resources being devoted to the incremental and breakthrough portions of the portfolio. With such an approach, a company would always be stretching for that radical idea that could completely disrupt their industry and enable the company to dramatically increase market share, while acknowledging that radical innovation is hard and risky, and should not be pursued to the exclusion of everything else.

Before you start working on radical innovation projects, here are some crucial questions you should look into before moving forward:

- Do you have the full support of top executives?

    You need top management support to make innovation happen. With radical innovation the support must go even further. You need executives who are personally committed and willing to spend their political capital to do this in the right way. Furthermore, you need executives with the right mindset for and a strong understanding of innovation.

- Does your company have a corporate strategy with room for innovation?

    More and more multibillion-dollar companies need to develop billion-dollar growth every year to satisfy their stockholders. They often take an acquisition approach to fulfill this need for growth, which can lead to a reduced focus on internal innovation efforts, including radical innovation projects, even though it is often acknowledged that such radical innovation projects in the long term can help develop entirely new business platforms that can bring high growth. You need to consider whether the overall corporate strategy works well with innovation.

- Do you have the people who can execute radical innovation projects?

    You need a special breed of people to make radical innovation happen. Their traits and skills include optimism, passion, drive, curiosity, belief in change, talent for networking, and the ability to deal with—and win over—the many internal and external antibodies that will oppose the project. Most companies do not have the proper processes in place to identify and develop such people.

- Do you have the organizational processes and setup needed to make radical innovation happen?

Having the proper processes and setup we discussed in Chapter 4 will decrease the number and power of the corporate antibodies that will fight against anything that changes the status quo.

- Is the time right?

Most radical innovation projects take a long time—often three to seven years to grow from an idea to substantial revenues. The projects are usually started when times have been good for at least a couple of years and you dare to invest, but your executives will start to hesitate as good times come to an end. They will be forced to take a hard look at the portfolio of innovation projects. There is a great risk of shutting down the more radical projects because it can be difficult to justify the high level of risk that comes along with the potential success.

Of course, it will come as no surprise that these are all questions you should ask when approaching open innovation. For some organizations, open innovation itself will be a radical step. So you have to make sure you are really ready for it.

⚷ Key Chapter Takeaways

- Companies that are in the early stages of establishing their innovation capabilities may be biting off more than they can chew if they pursue radical innovation because:
  - It can take too long to produce results.
  - In most organizations, few people on any level have successful experiences with radical innovation.
  - Projects that are somewhere in the range between incremental and radical innovation are more acceptable to risk-averse executives and managers.
  - It's easier to achieve radical innovation by buying a start-up and integrating it into your company.
  - Market-leading companies prefer to play it safe rather than cannibalizing and reinventing themselves.
- To pursue radical innovation successfully, companies must:
  - Have a corporate strategy with room for radical innovation and adequate time to implement that strategy.
  - Have people who can execute radical innovation projects and processes in place to make them happen.

PART III

PERSONAL LEADERSHIP FOR OPEN INNOVATION

Becoming an outstanding innovation leader, especially in a complex open innovation environment, is about more than just mastering the processes and techniques of innovation. You are expected to achieve critical organizational objectives in environments that are often fraught with big challenges, such as inadequate resources or internal resistance from people who prefer the status quo over change.

To succeed under such circumstances requires a special blend of traits that include optimism, passion, drive, curiosity, a belief that change can be good, the ability to deal with uncertainty, and good communication and networking skills. To become a great leader of open innovation also requires a mastery of certain personal skills that we will tackle in the final chapters of this book. These include:

- *Defining success:* To know whether you're achieving all that you're capable of as an innovation leader, you have to define what success will look like for you.
- *Identifying values:* You can only be successful in the long run if you know what really matters to you—your values.
- *Making change happen:* Once you've defined what success means to you, you may realize that to achieve your dreams, you'll need to make changes.

- *Managing time:* The innovation leaders I talk to frequently mention that they are struggling to manage their time so that they can achieve all that they want to achieve in their work while also having a fulfilling personal life.
- *Developing your personal brand and managing relationships:* Your network and relationships have a huge impact on what you do and what you can achieve. It starts with your values, as they define your personal brand, which again influence which kind of people want to connect with you.
- *Communicating your messages:* The ability to effectively communicate with a wide variety of stakeholders is essential for any leader of an open innovation effort. Whether it's a message about your personal brand or one about a project you are championing, you must know how to develop a value proposition and an elevator pitch that will get your message through to the stakeholders you want to influence.

In the chapters that follow, I discuss how these issues impact your ability to be an innovation leader or an entrepreneur, and I offer guidance on how you can master each issue. Let's start with determining what you believe success means.

CHAPTER

10

Defining Success

What is success? There is no short answer to that question, and everyone has an individual idea of what success means for them personally. That's why there are so many personal-development books on the topic. I have been discussing the meaning of success with innovation leaders for a long time, but an e-mail exchange a few years back helped me better understand what success really means to these people.

I had the e-mail exchange with Johnnie Rask Jensen, CEO and president of Danfoss Solutions, a corporate spinout from the Danfoss Group. If you ever get to meet Johnnie, you will know this is one heck of an intrapreneur. As a member of the INTRAP network, he sent me an e-mail following up on one of our previous meetings, in which I had given the participants the small task of reflecting on time. Most of the participants were late for that meeting, and as they called in with their estimated arrival times, I asked them to reflect on time as they made their way to the meeting. I remember how they smiled as we started the session, and one guy said it was the first time in a very long time that he had gotten the opportunity—and reason—to reflect on time. A good discussion followed.

Well, back to the e-mail from Johnnie. Here it is.

Hi Stefan,

Happy New Year and thanks for our cooperation in 2007. I have just renewed the membership for 2008 and I have had the time to reflect during the holidays. Some feedback. . . .

I think you touched upon something important during the meeting at Bang & Olufsen last time we met. My biggest resource challenge is not money, organization or such—it is, simply put, *time*, and I can see that the following issues have occurred during my job at Danfoss Solutions, which I did not worry much about earlier in my career:

- Continued education on a management level. I have neglected this very much in the past years, although it is important.
- Basic leadership skills during the daily work are not prioritized because we just do not have the time for it. It can be employee conversations, weekly meetings, ordinary social activities for the employees, the daily delegations (which could be better), and so on. These are things that seem like time-takers in the short run, but they are just the opposite in the long run. I wonder if others have the same feeling.
- The relationships with family and friends suffer due to the time spent at work and the isolation that an executive position creates. I sense that an executive position in a venture organization requires an even greater effort than an executive or management position in a more stable organization, which others also must have felt.
- Time to build and nurture business relationships is lacking (but here INTRAP gets into play . . . :)), but more specifically the time to nurture informal relationships within and outside the mother organization. This used to just be a natural part of the work, but today this is a challenge.
- Time to prioritize tasks and time to reflect in order not to lose the big picture and just focus on the daily fire fighting.
- Time to fight the doubt. There is no question that venture people are exposed to doubters, but how do we make sure that the doubt does not undermine our own organization?

. . . It could be interesting to hear how the other intrapreneurs think about this time issue or whether it is just me who feels this way.

Later,

Johnnie Jensen

President, Danfoss Solutions

Through my research and activities I know Johnnie is definitely not the only one stressed about finding time to do all the things he outlined in his message. Yet being a successful innovation leader means being able to set goals and get results that keep you moving forward, while having the time to reflect on and adjust to the longer course on which you are progressing.

Identifying your values goes hand-in-hand with defining what success means to you. Because defining your values is so important, I've devoted a separate chapter to it, but I want to stress here that you cannot achieve success without living in a way that is consistent with your values. Nevertheless, I will venture to guess that most of you do not even know your values. At workshops or in groups in which this topic pops up, I am always surprised to learn how many people have not given their personal values much thought. More on this critical topic in Chapter 11.

Pathways to Success

Too often, we let other people define what our success should be. Their expectations create illusions that you think you need to live by to be successful. We all know people who chose a college major or later a profession because that's what their parents expected of them. These are often some of the most unhappy and dissatisfied people around. To avoid allowing such mismatched expectations of success. you must develop your own definition of success.

Ideally, defining what success means to you is something you do early in your career, but it's never too late to do it. Some of the happiest people you'll ever meet are those who woke up and decided to make a change in midlife! By this stage, they truly know themselves and have developed the strength to do what makes them happy, instead of allowing others' expectations to limit them.

Working with innovation, we often talk about critical success factors. Have you considered developing your personal success factors? What should they be? To become successful as an innovation leader—and as a partner, family member, and friend—you can explore these pathways to success:

- Know your values.
     When you let others define what your success should be, it often causes internal conflict with your inherent values.

Even if you haven't taken time to delineate your values, you will feel stress when you take actions that go against them in an effort to please others. I assure you that knowing your values and living by them will help you eliminate this unfortunate situation.

- Follow your passion.

    As you get to know your values, you will also discover where your passion is. And you can only become successful in the true meaning of the word if you can live out your passion in the majority of your life. Passion is doing what comes naturally to you, and with a continued desire to learn and develop in this area. How do you let your passion out? How do you get the kicks that make life great? Why not plan for them?

- Decide on your personal vision.

    We all know how important it is for a company to set a vision that makes concrete the results the organization aims to achieve over the long term. Similarly, you can define your own personal vision that combines your values and your passion into a brief but meaningful statement of what you desire to achieve in business, in your personal life, and as a member of your community.

- Set goals.

    Once you've defined your vision, you can determine what short-range, mid-range, and long-term goals will get you there. Share your vision and goals with the people who are important in your life, to help build in accountability to your planning for success. Review your goals on a regular basis, making adjustments as you achieve progress or suffer setbacks. You will learn that working to the goals rather than achieving them is what makes you happy, so be prepared to set new goals when you reach your current ones.

- Understand and respect your stakeholders.

    Who will help you achieve your goals and personal vision? It's important to identify and understand your key influencers and what drives them. These are your stakeholders, and you must make sure they understand what you bring to the table and also how they can help you achieve success—and how you can help them become successful.

- Work on your T-Shape.

    Remember the T-Shape that I talked about back in Chapter 5? Go deep in at least one skill area and have breadth and empathy for other areas. Think of it as open innovation on a personal level—you need to accept that you don't know everything, and have the courage to seek help and advice from others. Gain a broader perspective by learning from those whose experiences and views differ from yours. If you have team members—either internally from your organization or externally from your open innovation partners—on whom you are relying to help you achieve your goals, be sure to share credit with them. Recognize the stakeholders in your personal life who make it possible for you to have the time needed to achieve success on your business goals; thank them for their role in your success.

- Stay current.

     While you're working toward your own set of goals, the outside world will not stand still. Make sure you keep on top of external developments that could impact your ability to achieve your vision.

- Communicate yourself.

     How do you want other people to look upon you? You might not like this, but it does not really matter much what you think of yourself. What really matters is how other people perceive you. Build and nurture your personal brand and work on your personal messages.

- Manage time.

     You might think that working hard for 60, 70, or 80 hours each week is what it takes to be successful. You might even think being a workaholic is a badge of honor. I have met many innovation leaders and intrapreneurs who think like this. But in recent years, some found reasons to reconsider how to manage and spend their time. One guy had a heart attack. Several people got divorced. Some realized that they were going through life without seeing their kids grow up. They got to the other side where they understood they needed to manage their time rather than letting time manage them.

Success Exercise

This is a short exercise that I've used in workshops to help people define what success means to them. You can do this exercise for yourself, but it would be great if you could discuss your answers with others. Perhaps even a group of innovation leaders and intrapreneurs who know what you are dealing with.

1. Think of three successful moments in business and in private life. Try to describe each of them, and try to define what the success looked like by using keywords.
2. Identify the reasons for success by using keywords.
3. Using the keywords, write one sentence that states what you need to focus on in order to be successful.

To provide you with more mental fodder as you start on your journey toward defining what success means to you, here are some inspiration quotes on the subject:

> *Success is a journey, not a destination.*
>
> —BEN SWEETLAND
> author and newspaper columnist

> *The fastest way to succeed is to look as if you're playing by other people's rules, while quietly playing by your own.*
>
> —MICHAEL KORDA
> book editor and author

> *Only those who dare to fail greatly can ever achieve greatly.*
>
> —ROBERT F. KENNEDY
> U.S. senator

Applied Good Sense—Personal Visions and Profits Aligned

Sanjoy Ray, Ph.D., founded and directs the Technology Innovation team in the MRL Information Technology, Technology and Applications Services group of Merck. Here he talks about his personal vision and how it is brought to life in his workplace.

What is your mission at Merck?

Ray: Our mission is to drive evidence-based investment decisions. This we do by finding innovative new information technologies, establishing positive relationships with the innovators behind them, and, orchestrating fast, collaborative experiments where the technology is tested in real MRL business scenarios.

The beauty of this approach is that we explicitly do not deliver capability. This ensures that we are free to determine the real truth about the capability, and so avoid being forced into making something work at all costs—an all-too-real situation for many who deliver IT capabilities. In fact, the experimental systems we use are deliberately decommissioned at the conclusion of each experiment, which typically lasts for three months. What we do deliver is an experimental outcome that drives unambiguous go/no-go investment decisions. Hard to imagine a better job, isn't it?

I know that you are driven by a personal vision. Can you share this with us?

Ray: Yes. Each and every one of us are patients at some time, and so is everyone we have ever cared about. I believe that a much larger part of their suffering will be preventable in future. I believe that the pharmaceutical industry will benefit patients in part by increasing the pace of scientific discovery using emerging information capabilities that are revolutionary in comparison to those in existence today. Furthermore these next-generation capabilities can be delivered by orchestrating the appropriate collaborations with brilliant best-of-breed innovators to leverage the breathtaking profusion of innovative IT outside pharmacology. I believe that the realization of these capabilities will help our industry to reduce suffering from unmet medical needs by the faster, cheaper, and safer development of new therapeutics.

How did you arrive at your personal vision? What was your process for developing it?

Ray: When I was given the opportunity to create the group, I was given very free rein to determine its direction. There were two major questions:

How would we do things right? This was the first question and the answer would lead us to develop a formal operating model based on the scientific method.

How would we do the right things? This was the second question, the answer to which was altogether unclear at the inception of the group.

(continued)

While seeking to answer this second question, I was led to try to understand the challenges of our industry and their causes, and so to understand what new capabilities will be needed to drive progress. Only when I understood that could I arrive at a rationale for decisions on which technologies we would work with and which we would not.

How do you make this happen at work?

Ray: The group has enjoyed considerable success, and a large part of that has been because we have both done things right and done the right things.

There are a number of key success factors:

First and foremost, I can't tell you how proud I am of the group I am privileged to lead. It's one thing for a leader to have a vision and an aspiration. It's quite another to deliver value based on it, and that's what this group does so effectively, day in and day out. So the critical success factor that differentiated our group was the ability of the team to deliver execution-focused innovation via excellently run experiments with defined outcomes. These folks are so phenomenally talented that they make this enormously complex process look easy.

Let me emphasize this point because it is so important: defining strategy, having the vision—I think those are the easy bits. The really tough part is the flawless execution that translates the strategy and vision into tangible value. So that makes me the least important part of the group, doesn't it? And that's how it should be. My job is to find the right people, create the environment where they can stretch and take risks, find them opportunities, give them what they need, and then get out of the way and watch the magic happen!

I have to say that the quality of the employees at Merck is really very high. I come from an academic background gained at such places as Imperial College London, Harvard, and the Whitehead Institute/MIT. Honestly, I can tell you that there are many at Merck who match or exceed the quality of the people at those institutions. We hire the best. Before I was given the opportunity to form the group, I recall wondering what these people could do if they were really "set free" to just achieve. So in a sense, forming this group was an experiment to test this hypothesis and prediction. The result is clear from the success of this group. It really helps for the leader to *not* be the smartest person in the group! That's not difficult at a company like Merck.

I would say that the other critical success factor is one I often see overlooked elsewhere. Simply put, the group acts always to make others successful and to align experiments with what really excites the various participants. We have found that if we operate in this way, there is extraordinary performance just from the enthusiasm and sheer goodwill of the participants. Acting in this way is much easier said than done, which is probably why it is far from common.

What are the pros and cons of being driven by a personal vision?

Ray: I think a very clear pro is the immense satisfaction of seeing each day's progress in the context of the vision, and knowing that the work of the day has gone towards lessening suffering, even if it is only a small step along the way. We are all patients! You, and more importantly, everyone you care about, are guaranteed at some time to be a patient. Think about it! That's very powerful and makes it easy to remain positive in the face of the many challenges that inevitably arise during any reasonably complex endeavor.

So being able to draw the line-of-sight linkage to what's really important is an excellent motivator that puts any challenge into its proper context. Think of your very worst challenge at work. However bad it is, can it possibly compare to that which is faced by a four-year-old patient in a pediatric oncology ward who is suffering through chemotherapy, and by her family who must watch helplessly as she suffers?

I can't see any cons in the environment I am in at Merck. It's perfect for fostering the kind of things we do.

Does your boss know you are more driven by a personal vision than profits? Have you had any clashes on this?

Ray: Yes, he does and he is very supportive, so there aren't any clashes about vision and motivation—he has a young family as do I! Senior leadership support is immensely important for anything so out of the norm as innovation. My boss, his boss, and other senior leaders have consistently provided critical support, for example, in providing air-cover while the group was being formed but was not yet productive. For this I am profoundly grateful. I find it all the more remarkable because there are so many competing demands for resources that one can always find a deserving home for funds, so there are, consequently, many temptations to take the easy way out and decommission something as risky and unknown as a new innovation group. So it took courage and faith from the leadership.

(continued)

However, I should add that this is perhaps not so surprising at Merck, whose former president, George W. Merck, said in 1951 that, "Medicine is for the people. It is not for the profits. The profits follow, and if we have remembered that, they have never failed to appear."

What is your advice to others who want to work in a competitive work-environment while staying true to their vision?

Ray: I would say they need to position themselves in a work environment where at least a substantial part of their personal vision is aligned with that of the institution. That's definitely the simplest path forward and the one that is most likely to lead to positive outcomes. If you spend so much time and invest so much energy in any endeavor (hopefully a good definition of work!), why would you be at any place where there isn't a match? What a waste.

As regards hypercompetitive environments, I would imagine that internal competition if taken to extremes is actually counterproductive because it leads to localized success at the expense of failure of the wider organization. Frankly, acting to make others successful could itself be a competitive advantage in such environments, simply because so few others would be acting in a way that leads to superior outcomes. As the saying goes: "In the land of the blind, the one-eyed man is king!"

🔑 Key Chapter Takeaways

- To fulfill your role as innovation leader to the greatest degree possible, you must define success, know how to make change happen, identify your values, manage relationships and time, and communicate your messages.
- The key pathways to your success include:
  - Following your passion.
  - Setting your personal vision and then identifying the goals that help you achieve it.
  - Identifying the people who will help you achieve your vision and building mutually beneficial relationships with them.
  - Working on your T-shape and keeping abreast of external developments that affect your personal vision and goals.
  - Building and communicating your personal brand and messages.
  - Managing your time.

CHAPTER 11

Know Your Values

I am puzzled that so few people can describe the values that guide their daily actions. Think about it. These are the fundamentals that help you become successful as an innovation leader or as an intrapreneur, as well as in your personal life. No doubt some of you have spent time helping your company define its core values, which, if followed, will drive the organization toward success. Doesn't it make sense to also define the core values that will impel you to success, as well? I want you to think more about this and start working on developing a better understanding of your values.

We all have values, whether we are consciously aware of them or not. Values are traits, qualities, or beliefs that we find valuable. According to Susan A. Heathfield, a human resources expert and consultant who writes for About.com, values "represent your highest priorities and deeply held driving forces."[1]

Furthermore, personal values are implicitly related to choice; they guide your decisions by allowing you to compare the values associated with each choice. I find this useful in this world of ours where we often seem to be condemned, rather than blessed, by choices. This is perhaps particularly true for people working in the field of innovation, which can be likened to the candy store of the corporation. With so many exciting and appetizing choices in front of you, how will you know what to choose if you aren't prepared to make values-based decisions?

Heathfield believes your values are made up of everything that has happened to you in your life and include influences from your parents and family, your religious affiliation, your friends and peers, your education, your reading, and more. You can argue that personal values developed early in life may be resistant to change. However, some values evolve due to external circumstances, and values can, in fact, change over time. As Heathfield advises, "you should recognize these environmental influences and identify and develop a clear, concise, and meaningful set of values, beliefs and priorities."[2]

Whether you've defined them or not, values impact every aspect of your life. We've all been in situations where we felt uneasy about what we were being asked to do. This means the action being asked of us is not aligned with our values. At such times, if you have defined your values, it is much easier to recognize the problem and to extricate yourself from the situation than if you haven't taken time to specifically identify the values that drive you. You become empowered to do what's best for you by being clear on your values.

My Values

Let me share my personal values with you. They are passion, trustworthiness, integrity, and the willingness to help others. I need to be passionate about what I am doing, because I believe this is the only way to become very good at what I am doing and to continuously enjoy what I do over the years. Passion makes things so much easier as you become more engaged and effective when you do what you really love to do. Hopefully, what you do also has a financial potential. I really try to find the passion in whatever I do.

Trustworthiness is important to me because I want to build relationships with people whom I can trust, and I want to have them trust me. Of course, this is a two-way function that is often forgotten by some people. In the long run, people who aren't trustworthy do not achieve success in either their business or personal lives.

Integrity is hard to describe, and yet it is quite simple. Integrity's primary definition in the dictionary is "the quality of possessing and steadfastly adhering to high moral principles or professional standards." But two secondary definitions are also informative: "Integrity is the state of being complete or undivided" and "the state of being sound or undamaged." Taken as a whole, these three definitions indicate that if we act with integrity, we will be whole and sound.

How does one put this into action? This is where I use my stomach and gut. If I really try to feel something, then I know what the right answer is or what the right thing to do is. Does a given thing feel right in my stomach? Can I feel the passion in myself and among the other people involved? Is there a strong element of trust involved? If not, I walk away. Intuition, which is interconnected with integrity, can be trained, so try to trust your intuition more often. Integrity comes when you are committed to follow this gut feeling. Not just once in a while and not always (no one is perfect), but very close to always. I believe integrity has become necessary to survive in a world that is becoming so small while presenting more options than ever.

The willingness to help and to be there for others is a double-edged sword for me. I live this value out to a very high extent in my business life. I always try to help others without expecting anything in return. I have learned this works well in the long run, and it cannot be separated from my networking mindset. In my personal life, this is more complicated. I know I can give more to people in my close circle, but sometimes I just don't. Perhaps I feel more comfortable with my family and friends, so I do not have to make the same effort. Perhaps I have used all my mental capacity for this value at work. I sense this is a mistake, and I am working to correct this.

I believe you can only be successful in the long run if you know your values and if you know what really matters to you. Furthermore, you need to live in a way that is consistent with your values. By sharing my values, I hope I can inspire you to start thinking about your own values.

Classification of Strengths

You can define values and strengths in many different ways. Perhaps you have developed your own definitions as I just did, or perhaps you prefer to use generally accepted definitions. For the latter, you should look further into the work done by the VIA Institute of Character. This nonprofit has developed a classification of strengths, as you can see below. They have also developed exercises that you can use to determine your own strengths.

The VIA Classification of Character Strengths

1. Wisdom and Knowledge—Cognitive strengths that entail the acquisition and use of knowledge.
   - Creativity (originality, ingenuity): Thinking of novel and productive ways to conceptualize and do things; includes artistic achievement but is not limited to it.
   - Curiosity (interest, novelty-seeking, and openness to experience): Taking an interest in ongoing experience for its own sake; finding subjects and topics fascinating; exploring and discovering.
   - Judgment and Open-Mindedness (critical thinking): Thinking things through and examining them from all sides; not jumping to conclusions; being able to change one's mind in light of evidence; weighing all evidence fairly.
   - Love of Learning: Mastering new skills, topics, and bodies of knowledge, whether on one's own or formally; obviously related to the strength of curiosity but goes beyond it to describe the tendency to add systematically to what one knows.
   - Perspective (wisdom): Being able to provide wise counsel to others; having ways of looking at the world that make sense to oneself and to other people.
2. Courage—Emotional strengths that involve the exercise of will to accomplish goals in the face of opposition, external or internal.
   - Bravery (valor): Not shrinking from threat, challenge, difficulty, or pain; speaking up for what is right even if there is opposition; acting on convictions even if unpopular; includes physical bravery but is not limited to it.
   - Perseverance (persistence, industriousness): Finishing what one starts; persisting in a course of action in spite of obstacles; "getting it out the door"; taking pleasure in completing tasks.
   - Honesty (authenticity, integrity): Speaking the truth but more broadly presenting oneself in a genuine way and acting in a sincere way; being without pretense; taking responsibility for one's feelings and actions.
   - Zest (vitality, enthusiasm, vigor, energy): Approaching life with excitement and energy; not doing things halfway or halfheartedly; living life as an adventure; feeling alive and activated.
3. Humanity—Interpersonal strengths that involve tending and befriending others.

- Capacity to Love and Be Loved: Valuing close relations with others, in particular those in which sharing and caring are reciprocated; being close to people.
- Kindness (generosity, nurturance, care, compassion, altruistic love, "niceness"): Doing favors and good deeds for others; helping them; taking care of them.
- Social Intelligence (emotional intelligence, personal intelligence): Being aware of the motives and feelings of other people and oneself; knowing what to do to fit into different social situations; knowing what makes other people tick.

4. Justice—Civic strengths that underlie healthy community life.
   - Teamwork (citizenship, social responsibility, loyalty): Working well as a member of a group or team; being loyal to the group; doing one's share.
   - Fairness: Treating all people the same according to notions of fairness and justice; not letting personal feelings bias decisions about others; giving everyone a fair chance.
   - Leadership: Encouraging a group of which one is a member to get things done and at the time maintain time good relations within the group; organizing group activities and seeing that they happen.

5. Temperance—Strengths that protect against excess.
   - Forgiveness and Mercy: Forgiving those who have done wrong; accepting the shortcomings of others; giving people a second chance; not being vengeful.
   - Modesty and Humility: Letting one's accomplishments speak for themselves; not regarding oneself as more special than one is.
   - Prudence: Being careful about one's choices; not taking undue risks; not saying or doing things that might later be regretted.
   - Self-Regulation (self-control): Regulating what one feels and does; being disciplined; controlling one's appetites and emotions.

6. Transcendence—Strengths that forge connections to the larger universe and provide meaning.
   - Appreciation of Beauty and Excellence (awe, wonder, elevation): Noticing and appreciating beauty, excellence, and/or skilled performance in various domains of life, from nature to art to mathematics to science to everyday experience.

(continued)

- Gratitude: Being aware of and thankful for the good things that happen; taking time to express thanks.
- Hope (optimism, future-mindedness, future orientation): Expecting the best in the future and working to achieve it; believing that a good future is something that can be brought about.
- Humor (playfulness): Liking to laugh and tease; bringing smiles to other people; seeing the light side; making (not necessarily telling) jokes.
- Religiousness & Spirituality (faith, purpose): Having coherent beliefs about the higher purpose and meaning of the universe; knowing where one fits within the larger scheme; having beliefs about the meaning of life that shape conduct and provide comfort.

What's Next?

Once you've defined your core values, the next step is to consider how well you're able to live by those values in your current position within your current company and in the open innovation environment in which you'll be developing relationships with numerous outside stakeholders. Does there appear to be any imbalance between your values and those of the people you're working with or the values of the top leaders of the company? You don't have to have a list of their personal values in front of you to know this. You can make this judgment based on their actions. It is not unusual for team members or executives to act in ways that aren't in sync with the company's expressed core values. All too often, the core values are just words on paper with no real commitment behind them.

Many people tell me they feel as though they're role-playing at work. If you frequently feel that you have to don a new persona the minute you cross the threshold at work, this is a sign that you're not able to live your values in your current business environment. If that's the case, take a step back and imagine what a workplace in which you could live your values would be like. Write down a description of how you'd be able to act in that ideal workplace. Realize that you have the potential to become better and to achieve greater success by being true to yourself and to your values.

Key Chapter Takeaways

- Your ability to achieve success is linked to having a clearly defined set of values that drive the choices you make in your work and personal life.
- Taking time to reflect upon and define your values is an invaluable exercise.
- It is important that your values and those of the organization in which you work be aligned. Otherwise, you will be forced into the uncomfortable position of role playing at work with little chance of achieving your career goals.
- Living each day in a way that is consistent with your values clears your path to success.

CHAPTER 12

Making Change Happen

Quite often when the innovation leaders and intrapreneurs I work with do the work of defining what success means to them, they come to the realization they will need to either change positions within their current company or find a new position elsewhere to achieve the career goals that are part of their definition of success. Sometimes they also decide they need to make changes to improve their work-life balance. These career development issues often evolve around what you might call the professional midlife crisis that can be caused by situations such as these:

- You have plateaued in your company with no obvious next step available to you that will move you forward on the career path you desire.
- Having defined your personal values, you realize they do not match those of your employer.
- You do not have the flexibility in your current position that will enable you to achieve a greater work-life balance.
- Your company is not focused enough on innovation to offer you the types of exciting innovation leadership or intrapreneurial opportunities you desire.
- You would like to serve on a board of directors with another company or take a leadership role in an industry organization to broaden your impact.

Resolving these situations requires bringing about significant change. Your ability to make the necessary change is usually rooted in two things: perceptions and relationships. Many people think their own perception of who they are matches the way other people see them. It is remarkable how often this is wrong. More importantly, when it comes to making the change you desire, you often give more weight to others' perceptions of you than you do to your own perception of yourself. Therefore, it is a good exercise to get a better understanding of how other people view you before you lock in on the things you want to change in your life. It might be that it is not you who have to change, but rather the perceptions other people have of you that need to change.

Change has much to do with perceptions and relationships, which can be seen in the cases of two innovation leaders who approached me for help in making change happen for them as they looked for new external career development opportunities:

Our first person, let's call him Peter, was about 50 years old and had spent 17 years in the same company, in positions with considerable leadership responsibility. He was seeking new opportunities because the situation with his current company was quite turbulent due to ownership issues. We started a process in which Peter identified his main areas of professional interests (skills, functions, and type of companies), his goals for personal development, and his aspirations for a better work/life balance. The next step was to look into his perception balance (own perception versus others' perceptions) and then to look into our combined relationships with a short list of five to ten companies that could be of interest to him.

The other person, let's call him Simon, was close to retirement. He had been with one company for the past 25 years and had seen it grow from a garage-size operation to a big business. He had been in charge of business development and was now looking for ways to use his experience by serving as on the boards of growth companies. The main challenge he presented me with was that he did not know how to activate his network. To some extent he hoped people would approach him, which did not happen. Achieving his goal required repeated action and persistence from Simon. Unfortunately, we did not get many results; it is especially difficult to get interesting board-of-director positions in times of financial turmoil.

Neither Peter nor Simon had given much thought to their perception balance, that is, how well their self-perception matched how others viewed them. Thus, they were unaware of others' perceptions that might interfere with their ability to achieve their goals. However, given their ages, they each might well have faced age discrimination as they tried to move toward their new goals, despite their personal self-images as men with much to offer. There could be other ways in which their personal perceptions might have differed from those of the people whose help they were going to need in bringing about changes in their lives. In addition, neither Simon nor Peter had worked on building and staying connected with his network in a strategic, that is, goal- and action-oriented, way. They were not as connected as they thought they were.

You too need to consider your perception balance. Take a hard look at yourself, and ask yourself whether there are people or incidents that can confirm the image you have of yourself. You will get some inspiration about how to do this when we get to Chapter 14 on personal branding. Now let us look into ways of bringing about change.

Five Steps to a Change Strategy

Everyone needs a personal strategy for change. Based on my work with innovation leaders and intrapreneurs, here are five steps to help you develop your change strategy:

1. Realize and acknowledge your issues—and choose to change.

    It is quite simple. Only you can make changes in your life, and it starts with opening your eyes to the differences between your current situation and the values and picture of success that you've developed for yourself.

    Here's something I hear a lot: "I am too old for change" or "Change is too difficult." You only need to look at any of the famous examples of people who achieved success relatively late in life to know that the first statement is not true. The second statement is undoubtedly true—change is indeed often difficult—but that never means it's impossible. Also, it is every bit as difficult to continue on the path you're following, even though that path has little chance of leading to the definition of success you've set out for yourself, as it is to change your life.

    The reality is that you always have a choice; you just need to realize and acknowledge the issues that are holding you back and choose to make the required changes. Among the changes that might help you move forward is the argument by American urban studies theorist Richard Florida that the choice of the place you live is one of the most important choices you can make. In *The Rise of the Creative Class* and *Who's Your City?*, he argues that the choice of where we live is the factor that is most predictive of our personal happiness. By choosing to live where creative people cluster, you may increase your ability to achieve change and become part of a force that drives innovation.

I would argue that choosing the organization you work for based on how well its values match the values you want to live by is similarly important to achieving success and happiness. If there is a mismatch in values, this should be a strong motivation for finding a new employer that is a better fit.

Here are other questions to ask yourself about your work environment to determine if it is a good match for you or whether you need a change:

- Do you feel passionate about the company's vision and mission?
- Do you like the people you work with? Do you share the same values?
- Do you feel a need to be a different person at work from what you are when away from work?
- Do you often compromise your own values in order to get things done?
- Does senior management think long term and support innovation and change, or are they mostly focused on quarter-to-quarter financial results?
- Do you have the resources necessary to push innovation forward?

You could consider testing whether you are in the right company by setting the stakes a bit high. Imagine that you have an ongoing case where you continue compromising your values. What would happen if you put your job at risk to make this right? Are you a valued employee that your company really wants to keep, or will they let you go and ignore that they have an employee willing to fight for something he/she believes is worthwhile? Be careful with this test; you might get what you ask for.

In our world of seemingly unlimited choices, part of your change-making strategy must include developing the ability to say no. You will need to eliminate some choices after carefully evaluating them and concluding that they won't take you to the success you desire. However, other people—who may not be aware of your values or your definition of success—may pressure you to say yes to things that aren't in your best interest. At such times, being able to look at the situation with clear eyes and eliminate outside influences is essential, as is the ability to firmly but politely refuse to be pulled in directions in which you don't want to go.

2. Understand the difference between push and pull when it comes to change.

You may be either pushed or pulled to create change. You might decide to pull change toward you by proactively choosing to have a mentor, coach, or friend help you work on the change you wish to create. Or you may be pushed to react to factors external to you.

Once you realize and acknowledge your issues, you might feel things are under control and that you are in charge of the problems caused by your issues. I used to believe this. For many years I worked on issues such as an occasionally hot temper, impatience with people who cannot follow my ideas, and mood changes. I used to think, "Yes, I have some issues, but at least I know of them and I am working on them." I did make progress, but it was quite slow. Things did not really change until I had an unexpected external push that forced me to take a hard look at myself and realize what I could lose if I did not make the necessary changes. This push was from the personal part of my life, but the pattern is similar in professional and career development.

I have helped many innovation leaders and intrapreneurs with skill- and career-development issues. It usually goes like this. At first, there is a lot of build-up with very little action. This can last for years. Then something happens. A few people manage to create a pull effect by understanding that they need help, and so they reach out for that help. The external feedback makes it easier to see the full picture and understand that more is needed to make change happen. Then they move forward with actions mentioned later.

More often, it is an external push. It could be that the future becomes uncertain because of major organizational restructuring process. You might get a new boss or a new board of directors. You might even lose your job. Pressure piles up, and some people frown. But your experiences as an innovation leader or intrapreneur have heightened your threshold. You are accustomed to pressure, and you understand that such an external push can be turned around for something positive.

The most important thing about external involvement is that it can help give you the impetus to act. As author Anthony Robbins points out, people will change when the pain of staying in the status quo becomes greater than the pain of leaving.

3. Set goals.

You will need to set change goals and determine how to measure your progress. A good place to begin is to write out the reasons why you want to change. Next, develop your goals for change and the detailed action steps that will take you there. Finally, you need some way to measure your progress, both in the short-term and over the long haul. Set metrics that you can check in with periodically to make sure you're moving in the right direction.

This could go hand-in-hand with the vision and goal-setting work discussed in Chapter 10. On a cautionary note, make sure your goals are realistic. Don't complicate things too much by having too many goals and not enough priorities. Better to make slow, steady progress in one or two key areas than to get weighted down with so many goals that the burden becomes overwhelming and nothing really happens. As Carmine Coyote writes in his blog, "Slow Leadership," "When everything is important, nothing is. You must prioritize or increase the risk of failure. Focus on what truly matters most—just one thing, if possible—and get it done. Then move on to the next. Success breeds success."[1]

4. Build accountability into your change effort—and begin to change other's perceptions of you—by communicating your goals to key stakeholders.

This is similar to the dynamics of good teams. They work well because the team members keep each other mutually accountable while having a sincere concern for each other. Most likely, you are not comfortable telling everyone about your issues, but it would help greatly to be able to tell someone you trust in order for them to be able to act as good team members in helping you reach your goals.

There are also reasons to tell a broader audience. As I've already discussed, whether you like it or not, the world does not revolve around what you believe about yourself. Other people's perceptions of you can affect your ability to change. By conveying to others that you're working on making changes, you can help begin to change perceptions that are working against you. This in turn can make it easier to reach your goals

5. Create rituals to enforce change.

Research into how people change existing habits and form new ones suggests that many people do not have the self-discipline that change requires. Yet some people do make significant changes in their lives.

There are many reasons for recommending the book *Happier: Learn the Secrets to Daily Joy and Lasting Fulfilment* by Tal Ben-Shahar; his discussion on change is just one of them. On change, Ben-Shahar points to a book by Jim Loehr and Tony Schwartz entitled *The Power of Full Engagement,* in which they suggest a way of thinking about change: "They suggest that instead of focusing on cultivating *self-discipline* as a means towards change, we need to introduce *rituals.* According to Loehr and Schwartz, 'building rituals requires defining very precise behaviours and performing them at very specific times—motivated by deeply held values.'"[2]

Experts generally advise introducing no more than one or two rituals at a time, and making sure they become habits before introducing new ones. Incremental change is more likely to succeed than expecting vast change to occur overnight. One only has to look at people who make a New Year's resolution to go to the gym every single day versus someone who sets a more reasonable goal of gradually increasing their gym use from one day to two days and then to three days a week. Nevertheless, both goals have to start by going to the gym, and this could be set as a ritual.

According to Ben-Shahar, "People are sometimes resistant to the idea of introducing rituals because they believe that ritualistic behaviour may detract from spontaneity or creativity—especially, when it comes to interpersonal rituals such as a regular date with one's spouse, or artistic rituals such as painting. However, if we do not ritualize—or plan—activities . . . we often don't get to them, and rather than being spontaneous, we become reactive (to other's demands on our time and energy). More important, we can integrate spontaneity into a ritual, for example, deciding spontaneously where we go on the ritualized date."[3]

⚷⚓ Key Chapter Takeaways

- Your ability to change the trajectory of your career depends on two factors:
  1. The balance between how you view yourself and how others view you.
  2. The relationships you have built.
- If there is a perception imbalance, you can change it by:
  - Realizing and acknowledging your issues and committing to change.
  - Understanding the difference between push and pull when it comes to change.
  - Setting goals and prioritizing them.
  - Building accountability into your change effort—and beginning to change others' perceptions of you—by communicating your goals to key stakeholders.
  - Creating rituals to enforce change.

CHAPTER 13

Managing Time

As an innovation leader, you are bound to have time issues. This career is time-consuming. You are being pulled from all directions, and no matter how many items you cross off your to-do list, the number of tasks just seems to keep increasing. And as we move toward open innovation, time management becomes even more of an issue as you have to juggle more relationships and most likely deal with people around the world in different time zones that will put even more pressure on your work time.

Time—or more likely the lack of it—is something we often get into during our network meetings because all of our members spend most of their time in a little box labeled *urgent*. We have a general tendency to assume there's nothing we can do about it; issues with time just go with the territory, right?

Well, that answer is only partially correct. The reality is that unless you get control of your time management issues, you stand little chance of making the type of change happen that was discussed in the Chapter 12. So here I'm going to touch on two principles that help us understand why managing time is such a challenge, and then I'll suggest that there are some things you can do to get more control over your time. First, let's look closely at where your time goes.

Analyze Your Time Budget

Many people run into financial trouble because they have never established a budget that sets spending priorities and allocates their money accordingly. They have trouble making it from paycheck to paycheck and are uncertain exactly where their money went. The same thing happens when you don't analyze where your time goes and set priorities. At the end of the day or the week, you realize you haven't completed important work tasks, have only made it to the gym once, and have spent very little time with your family or friends.

Where did the time go? You were ultra-busy all week long, but what did you accomplish that moved you toward your vision of success? I am no big fan of capturing a lot of data and overanalyzing what is going on, which is what most time management exercises are about. Smart people already have an idea of what is wrong and why. More often, they just need a quick overview and a push or pull effect as we discussed during the change chapter. So this is an exercise to help you get a quick overview of where your time goes so you can identify what kind of changes will give you more control over that most precious commodity—the hours of your life.

You could keep a detailed log of everything you do for the next week, noting how much time you spend on things such as work, friends and family, yourself, transportation, charity, and much more. However, as only very few of us have the discipline to keep such a log, I suggest that you aim for the big picture and spend 30 minutes reflecting on how you spend your time. First, review the questions below, and then reflect before you start answering them. Use keywords only for your answers.

How do I communicate (meetings, phone, e-mail) with others? Do I even have to interact with these people? What would happen if I cut meetings in half? What if I decided to communicate by e-mail first, then by phone, and only if necessary have meetings?

Reflections (only keywords: _____

_____

What kind of activities would I like to spend less time on? Why do I spend time on things I do not like to do? What would happen if I did not do them? Could someone else do them for me?

Reflections (only keywords) _____

_____

What kind of activities would I like to spend more time on? Why am I not spending more time on these activities?

Reflections (only keywords)_____

_____

Where and when am I wasting time? What can I do to stop wasting my time?

Reflections (only keywords)_____

_____

Where and when am I most productive? What can I do to create more slots in which I am highly productive?

Reflections (only keywords)_____

_____

You need to create a few action points to change things. Decide on three things you would like to change in the coming weeks. I suggest you keep it simple at first to get some early wins. You can always repeat this exercise.

Try using the sentence below to write down your actions.

"I want to change my (*insert behavior/issue*) by (*insert action*) because this will give me (*insert desired result*)."

This is a simple exercise that will not take much time. The purpose is to make you consider whether you spend time on the things that are important to you and whether you should start making changes to the way you handle your time management.

How Did Things Get This Way?

To understand why time management is such a challenge for most of us, we need to understand two principles:

- Parkinson's Law.
    This is the adage that "work expands so as to fill the time available for its completion." First put forth by British naval historian Cyril Northcote Parkinson in an essay in *The Economist*

in 1955 and later in a bestselling book called *Parkinson's Law: The Pursuit of Progress*, this principle explains why you—and the people you delegate to—rarely finish a task before its deadline.

Given 30 days to complete a report, we will research, research, and research some more before buckling down to write it in the last few days before the deadline. Yet if given two days to write the same report, we will manage to do all the research and writing within those two days. This also explains why so many people are seen in stores on Christmas Eve doing their shopping at the very last minute. Some of them are there looking for last-minute markdowns, but the majority are probably there because of Parkinson's Law.

Parkinson's Law is responsible for many of the mind-numbing meetings we all find ourselves in each week, and it explains why your time budget almost undoubtedly shows that you're spending vast amounts of time on non-priority issues.

- The 80/20 Rule.

The 80/20 Rule (also known as the Pareto principle) also can be applied to time management. Using this rule, we can say that 80 percent of effects come from 20 percent of the causes. In other words, 80 percent of your results come from 20 percent of your efforts, which means we all spend a lot of our time and energy on doing things that don't move us closer to our work or personal goals.

Being aware of the effects of Parkinson's Law and the 80/20 Rule can help you take a fresh look at your time budget to identify ways in which you could better manage your time. Answer these questions:

- Are there times when you stretch work out, doing more research or holding more meetings than necessary to make a decision, prepare a report, or otherwise move a priority forward?
- If you had to, could you realistically accomplish in four days what it now takes you five days to do? In other words, are there items on your to-do list that could be delegated or even dropped altogether without the world coming to an end?
- Are there items on your to-do list that could be outsourced to a virtual assistant? Think beyond your work life to your personal life. Are there tasks there that could be done by a

virtual assistant? Just Google "virtual assistant," and a whole world of possibilities will open up for you.

- Which 20 percent of your effort produces 80 percent of your results?
- Are there a lot of nonpriority tasks that could be bundled together to be accomplished in one quick burst of energy? For example, do you take time out to do one personal errand each day when you could actually combine five errands and get them all done in approximately the same amount of time that it previously took you to do one?

Create Thinking Time

When you have identified ways in which you could manage your time better, one of the top priorities for the freed-up time should be thinking. You work with innovation at a high level, and you need time to think and reflect to be as good as you can be. Very few of us manage to do this in today's hectic world, but with a few changes, you can probably free up one hour of time a week for high-value thinking. Once you try this, you'll think it's the greatest luxury of your week.

An hour of solitary reflection (with no interruptions for multitasking or other distractions allowed) could make a tremendous difference in your ability to remain focused on your vision and your priorities. To make maximum use of this valuable time, your thinking needs to be directed toward a particular issue. Here are some additional guidelines:

- Set an objective.
  What do you want to achieve with this hour?
- Fully define the problem first.
  Don't jump immediately to a solution before exploring all the facets of the issue at hand.
- Write, type, or record your thoughts ASAP.
  It's all too easy to forget your thinking and your conclusions if you move on after your thinking hour and don't get your ideas saved. Also, putting something on paper makes your commitment to it more concrete and is more likely to prompt you to actually follow through on a plan.
- Make maximum use of any solitary time.
  Many people note that they get their best ideas when walking or running or even driving alone. Any time you're

alone and away from interruptions can be good thinking time as long as you don't let your cell phone or Blackberry interfere. Just be sure you record your results as soon afterward as you can.

Putting Time Management into Action

I once sent an e-mail to the members of my Danish network groups. It was inspired by the book phenomenon, *The 4-Hour Work Week* by Timothy Ferris. What a title! That certainly helped make the book an international bestseller, and it also caught my interest as I was looking into how innovation leaders and intrapreneurs manage their time.

To be honest, I did not read the full book. It is a tad too superficial and gung-ho, but Ferris also deserves a lot of respect for creating entirely new ways of managing—and thinking about—your time. My e-mail to the network went like this:

Dear friends,

This evening you could have seen an interesting clip on TV. It was about how you could cut down on the time spent at work and get more time for the fun stuff in life: family, friends, and sports/leisure activities.

The clip was on Timothy Ferris, who has written *The 4-Hour Work Week* (www.fourhourworkweek.com/blog/). The book is typically American. Sometimes it just gets too much and too "just do it," but it also has golden nuggets waiting to be picked up.

It has been one of my inspirations for creating a more simple life, which has been one of my main tasks for the last six months. Among other things, the book helped me:

• Prioritize my contacts.

My prioritized way of communicating with others is (1) e-mail (2) phone (3) meetings. It has surprised some that I did not want to meet with them because I believed—and because it turned out—the task could be done by e-mail or phone. It is not to be rude. It just saves time for all involved, and it works fine. Don't worry—I do not plan to turn our network into a virtual community—it is great seeing you face-to-face :-).

- Outsource what can be outsourced.

You will be surprised to know what you can actually outsource in India—and other countries. Why not look further into those slightly dull and perhaps even time-constraining tasks you have? Perhaps they can be outsourced. Or what about those jobs for which a helping (virtual) hand would be just fine—at work and leisure? Think hard why it is that you cannot outsource them. I use or have used people in the United States (publications) and India (market research and web site development). It takes a while to find the right people, but I can definitely recommend that you look into freeing up time like this.

- Set aside time for my priorities.

Having two great girls, aged 3 and 6, takes time and commitment. Sports—triathlon for now—takes time and hard work. I have chosen to give my family and my sports high priority. It requires that I set aside time for these. Work has not been damaged by this—in fact, quite the opposite, because I find myself to be more focused and productive than I used to be.

I hope you can find some inspiration in this.
Best regards,
Stefan

I received many responses to this e-mail. First, people appreciated that I was being open and honest about things that were going on in my life; it seemed to strengthen my relationships with many of them. Also, many people reported that they had taken time to reflect on my message and were trying to do the things I suggested. Here's an interview that shows how and why one person took action from my message.

Meeting the Challenge of Managing Time

Henrik Solkær was Vice President for Innovation & Technology and Sustainable Development at Danisco Sugar during this interview. Henrik was later appointed to Senior Vice President for Corporate Innovation & Technology and Sustainable Development at Nordzucker AG, following the merger of the two companies.

(continued)

What are your biggest issues with regard to managing time?

Solkaer: I have a few issues. The first one is to make sure that I always prioritize the most important issues in order to be able to give full attention to situations that require it. It is necessary to be able to clear the calendar, and I have to do that sometimes.

I also really try to make sure that whatever I do is done as efficiently as possible. This is not just to save time but also to energize and create momentum for myself and around me. As a leader at Danisco Sugar, I work to build a culture in which we are cautious about time, decision-oriented, and dynamic. We aim for action.

My personal drive is to continue to move toward the priorities that I have in my life. It is similar to work because I try to use my time as cautiously as possible. I try not to waste time and to be as dynamic as possible when I go for my plans, goals, and dreams. This goes hand-in-hand with how I deal with time at work.

For the overall aspect, I think managing time is a big challenge. It is so easy not to spend it in the right way—and, thereby, lose focus, direction, and speed. However, having this kind of focus on time, it is important, too, sometimes, to just let go of control.

Letting go of control? Can you give some example of this?

Solkaer: I try to talk with colleagues whenever there is room for it. We just talk and let things happen. Sometimes I get an instant feeling that I need to let go. I realize it is time to just skip the agenda, to just be there and see what happens.

My e-mail gave you some inspiration about creating a four-hour work week. Which reflections did you make about this?

Solkaer: It was a big inspiration to look at some main things and it created some aspirations to be able to break some habits and thus save time. I believe that time is such a scarce resource, so I am a curious about listening to the messages of Timothy Ferris, the author of the book.

Which actions did you take?

Solkaer: I immediately changed my priorities about how to get in touch with people. E-mail first, then phone, and meetings as the last option. This helps me become even more cautious about how to set up my appointments.

Another thing is that whenever I go into a meeting, I suggest we try to halve the time allocated. This works, and now I also have this in mind when I plan my future meetings.

Now, a few weeks later, what has the results been after taking these actions?

Solkaer: Besides cutting time spent on meetings, I stay more focused and try to find the best and most efficient ways to organize things through delegation. I often ask myself how this can be done more easily.

I have to admit this is often seen from my perspective as my own cautiousness has grown. This has not really been an issue with others because I find that, the more you delegate, the more other people get involved in a good way. I think I delegate well and much, but I intend to do so even more.

I also got a reflection of my actions. You need to prioritize what you want and try to put it first. This goes for every day, week, and beyond. You really need to push it forward.

Did people notice your changed behavior? If yes, can you give some examples of how they reacted?

Solkaer: Yes, they noticed a change, and I think they got inspired and learned from me. My colleagues are, to a great extent, motivated to spent time more efficiently and using their resources carefully and optimally.

We actually nominated a person who will develop a range of ideas about how to improve performance and efficiency. This was inspired by your e-mail, which I brought into a strategy seminar held just after I got it. It was decided it was worthwhile looking into this and developing a range of ideas. We have also bought copies of *The 4-Hour Work Week*.

On learning, I believe that people feel inspired to become more efficient and to crack bad habits. I think everyone has a style of doing things and this becomes embedded in their way of work. One of our challenges is to change this approach. How can things be done better and faster without compromising quality? Not so many people challenge the status quo.

Have you seen a downside to prioritizing your means of communication (e-mail, phone, meetings)?

Solkaer: No, there have not been any negative side effects. I learned that sometimes you have to put time efficiency aside and try not to be too tense. Efficiency is not the only success criteria, because you should not compromise the quality of a solution or a decision. At the same time, efficiency is not an element of, for instance, a personal conversation or something similar.

(continued)

Do you plan any further actions about managing time?

Solkaer: I also would like to speed up the pace of making decisions and actions. This momentum of improving actions has an acceleration impact. The more decisions you make, the more momentum you get. It stimulates the surroundings and creates much energy, which very much affects our culture.

You have a leadership position within your company. Do you plan to influence others to make similar changes?

Solkaer: As a leader, I see my role as someone who should always improve our culture and our ways of doing things. I definitely see myself as someone trying to influence others around me.

I think one of the potential big boosters of time efficiency would be to reduce the orthodoxy of where you work and how many hours you work. I think it would make a difference if you could eliminate the number of hours you are required to work—for instance the formal 37 hours in Denmark—and instead just focus on the tasks that you have to do. Whatever time you win back, you can use as you decide.

This could free up a lot of time and stimulate a lot of creativity. Of course, this poses some severe organizational challenges, and you will, also, lose something when people do not meet as often. But it could, also, set off a lot of creativity.

⌐ Key Chapter Takeaways

- Take time periodically to reflect on how you're budgeting your time; make sure you're allocating this precious resource in ways that maximize your chances of achieving success.
- Control your time; don't let others control it for you.
- Keep Parkinson's Law in mind, and make sure you're not stretching tasks out longer than actually necessary. When delegating work to others, realize that they, too, will usually take the full amount of time you allot to complete a task, so set deadlines that are realistic but tight.
- Use the 80/20 Rule to evaluate where you get the most value from the time you spend. Make note of activities that are not pushing you toward success, and outsource or even eliminate them.
- Leverage the power of solitary reflection; set aside at least one hour each week to think deeply about a specific issue.

14

Polishing Your Personal Brand

I would argue that your skills are not your most attractive asset on the job market today. In this competitive world, they are merely table stakes. Your career today is no longer built just on what you know and what you can achieve. Today it is very much also about your personal brand and your network of relationships. This is especially true in an open innovation world, where having a strong, wide-ranging network and being viewed as a thought leader are key assets. I'll tackle relationships in the next chapter, but in this chapter we'll focus on your personal brand.

"My personal brand? Come on, I am who I am," you might say. Wrong. You are who other people believe you are, and this will determine how you can build and nurture the relationships that can define your career and determine whether you achieve your vision of success. Regardless of whether you know it or like it, you already have a personal brand. The people you work directly with and peers that you know throughout your industry all have perceptions about your experience and your capabilities.

I know talking about your personal brand is somewhat controversial and seen as manipulative in many countries, although less so in the United States. This creates even more incentive for us to deal with this subject in a straightforward manner—down to earth and applied in practical ways rather than flashy and fancy strategies. It also makes it even more important that you identify your values because there is nothing phonier than a personal brand or self-identify that is not coherent with one's values. I think we can agree that authenticity is a great asset today with regard to products and services. The same goes with you.

Once a perception of you—your personal brand—has been created, it is difficult to change. This works positively as well as negatively, so make sure you are aligned with your values and your future plans when you start actively working your personal brand.

Why Does It Matter?

Why should you care about personal branding? I have learned that an added focus on personal branding—and on building relationships that can help you leverage it—is an investment, not a cost. It creates freedom and new opportunities for you to do what you care about. If you have a strong, positive personal brand, you are more apt to:

- Receive interesting assignments or be given more freedom to choose what you'd like to do.
- Receive more recognition and better pay.
- Be given more opportunities to represent your company externally, which in turn might open up new career options outside your present job.

The purpose of polishing your personal brand is to get others to communicate the *right* message about you and your competences. It is also about expectations, opportunities, and rewards. You can't have success if you can't handle professional expectations. The people in your personal network base their expectations on your personal brand, your personality, and your skills.

When your network is well developed, your personal brand helps create your opportunities. No opportunities, no rewards. Simply put, your personal brand can define your career, so why not try to make the best of it?

Certainly, if you were launching a new product or service, you would spend considerable time considering how to define and polish its brand. Doing the same thing for your personal brand is really no different. You want to be visible to senior management, and you want them to understand your unique set of abilities and your capacity to help them achieve corporate goals. You want to make sure people are aware of your achievements and any new skills you've gained since you were first hired. You want to be known as someone who can uncover and solve problems, and someone who is persistent and willing to take on new opportunities. All of this can be done without coming across as too self-promotional or egotistical.

Of course, it's important to remember that polishing your personal brand is not enough. You must still continue to further develop your knowledge and other assets. Your career development ends quickly if you only think about milking your assets (your knowledge, brand, and network).

Role Models

Before we get into how to build your personal brand I would like you to think a bit about role models. What personal brands have you admired in other people?

Pick up to four people who inspire you and/or that you admire. Consider and answer the following questions:

- Why have you chosen exactly those people? List the values, qualities, and results that these people have achieved that cause you to admire them.
- What do role models mean to you—and what can you use role models for?
- What keywords would you use to describe your choices?

Is there a connecting thread in your choices that supports and/or identifies values and qualities that are important to you? Doing this analysis can help you better define what qualities you want to highlight in your personal brand.

Create Your Personal Brand

I work with two key steps in building a personal brand: create and communicate. In creating a brand, here are the parts you will need to explore:

1. The future. Define your strategic goals.
2. You about you. Become clear on your values and traits.

3. Others about you. Understand how other people see your values and traits.
4. Check your digital footprints. Google yourself.
5. Identify your unique contributions and define your personal brand statement.
6. Know your environment. Focus on competitors and influencers.

The Future—Your Strategic Goals

The most important part of creating your brand is something I really need to emphasize: you need to know what you want to achieve with your personal brand. There is no reason to start a lot of activities if you do not have an endgame in mind.

What are your goals in the short, medium, and long term?

	Short term (6–12 months)	Medium term (1–3 years)	Long term (more than 3 years)
Material goals (your pay, business growth)			
Career goals (status and authority, desirable jobs, respect in the business)			
Personal goals (other than the material goals and career goals)			

You about You

Once you have made a plan with your goals and an overview of things you want to change, you should get to know your values. If you've looked into the VIA Classification of Character Strengths mentioned in Chapter 11, you've already done the important groundwork.

How would you describe your own personality, your values, and your talents?

Questions 1–4 should be answered with single words, not sentences.

1. What traits and values are most pronounced in your personality?

   _____

   _____

   _____

   _____

2. What do you consider to be your greatest talents and qualities?

   _____

   _____

   _____

3. What are your professional interests?

   _____

   _____

   _____

4. What are your private interests?

   _____

   _____

   _____

5. How would you describe your professional self in one sentence?

   _____

   _____

Others about You

Do you know the current status of your personal brand? I suggest you get 360° views on how you are seen by people you work with and people in your network. Ask people who know you well to give a candid view of how they see you. If you do not want to risk shaking up your close relationships, you can do this with a coach or a network group. Although they might not know you as well as your closest circle of friends and business contacts, they will still know you well enough to give you valid feedback.

This feedback will help you identify any imbalance between what you believe your brand is and how others perceive you. You should also Google yourself to get an idea of the digital footprints you have left so far. You might be in for a surprise when you do this.

1. Once you get the feedback from your private and professional circles of acquaintances, you should compare it to your own views about you. Look out for patterns or certain tendencies in the answers from others.

Personal traits and values	Talents and qualities
Own answers	
Answers from others	

2. Write down any discrepancies between your answers and the answers of others, and their significance for your personal brand.

Discrepancies	Significance for your personal brand

3. You have now created an overview of your personal brand in the form of your personality, your values, and your talents.

   Is there anything you want to delete, change, or add to your personal brand? If so, how can you adjust your personal brand?

Adjustment of your personal brand	Possible action

Google Yourself

Search for yourself on Google. Do you show up on unexpected web pages? Is there anything that surprises you or confirms your expectations in relation to your personal brand?

_____

_____

_____

Your Personal Brand Statement

Your next step is to ask yourself a really tough question. What are the things you do that really make a difference in your work? You need to get into the things that make you proud and that you always bring up when people ask you what makes you a unique contributor. No, this is not about your team; it is about you as an individual. I am amazed how often people try to talk about their efforts in a team when I try to get an understanding of how they, as individuals, make a difference.

Unique contributions: _____

_____

_____

The answers to the preceding question leads to what you want to be known for. Assuming your answers are aligned with your values and goals, you can use this to create a personal brand statement on which to build further when you start communicating your personal brand.

You should not boast that you are the best innovation leader or intrapreneur in the world because you most likely aren't even close. The statement is just too broad considering the many people working in this field.

You need a more specific and concise niche, and you should also consider a specific audience. You should also make sure your niche is aligned with your passions and goals in order for it to be reflective and to last.

For your inspiration, my own personal brand statement is this: I help companies identify and develop the people who drive innovation. A person within my broader network could claim that he is an authority on user-driven innovation within medico-related companies and another person could claim that he is an expert on creating value out of services and knowledge in product-oriented companies. What is your personal brand statement?

Personal brand statement: _____

_____

_____

Think of this statement as your personal elevator speech. This is what you say when you have an opportunity to tell someone what you do. It will be much more of a conversation starter than just supplying your job title and your company name when you meet someone new, and it will make you much more memorable.

Know Your Environment

Personally, I do not care much about competition because I believe it is more important which value I can deliver to my network members and consulting clients rather than what my so-called competitors are up to.

However, this is a bit different in a larger organization because you always have to fight for resources, attention, and promotions.

However, as much as I hope you do not see your colleagues as cutthroat competitors, you still should know of—and in some cases map and observe—your internal and external competitors or colleagues with regard to their standing and influence in the organization. Needless to say, you should do the same with the people who can influence—positively or negatively—your road to success.

Try to get an understanding of the people you are analyzing, particularly regarding thier formal and informal status in the organization. Are they only leaders on the formal organizational chart, or do they manage to create a following around them? Are they visible in the organization? Are they good speakers, writers, or networkers? Try to get an idea of how they develop and leverage their internal and external relationships.

Try this exercise with three people now. Then start observing what happens in the organization, and add other people to your list when they inspire you or when someone gets an opportunity or promotion that surprises you.

You should also consider applying this to the ecosystem in your industry because this will help you get a better understanding of the dynamics, which could open up your eyes for opportunities you have not yet seen.

People to watch	Status	Visibility	Networks	Other observations

You need to consider the people you need in your network and the people who could have a negative influence on your career. Who are they? Why are they important? How can a relationship add value to both of you? How can you work around a negative influence? As your goals change, try to do this with a short-, mid-, and long-term perspective. Try the exercise with three people, and, if possible, try to select a person for the short-, mid-, and long-term perspective.

Who?	Why?	How?

Communicate Your Personal Brand

The second key step in building your personal brand is communicating it, and here I would like to introduce you to management guru and author, Tom Peters. He coined the term *personal branding* more than a decade ago when he wrote an article entitled "The Brand Called You" in *Fast Company* magazine.[1]

Tom Peters says it all matters. When you're promoting your personal brand, everything you do—and everything you choose not to do—communicates the value and character of your brand. Everything from the way you handle phone conversations, to the e-mail messages you send, to the way you conduct business in a meeting, is part of the larger message you're sending about your brand.

According to Tom Peters—and I agree—the key to any personal branding campaign is word-of-mouth marketing. Your network of friends, colleagues, clients, and customers is the most important marketing vehicle you've got; what they say about you and your contributions is what the market will ultimately gauge as the value of your brand. So the big trick to building your brand is to find ways to nurture your network of colleagues—consciously.

We will get further into networking on the personal level in Chapter 15. For now I will introduce you to a number of communication tools based on four categories: perform, write, speak, and meet.

Perform. This is how you do your work. You could call this the prerequisite for everything else because, if you do not perform well, all the rest really does not matter. You cannot hide underperformance or incompetence for very long.

The key to your performance regarding to personal branding is to get noticed for what you do by leaving an individual footprint on all teamwork and making sure you get the proper credit for your individual work. I do not suggest that you should kick and scream every time you are involved in a project to claim the credit you deserve, but you should observe whether the key people have noticed your contributions. If not, you should evaluate the situation and find ways of making this happen. More importantly, you should observe whether this is a common occurrence. If so, is it because you do not claim credit or because your colleagues or managers tend to outright overrun you and take all the credit?

As Tom Peters puts it: "One key to growing your power is to recognize the simple fact that we now live in a project world. Almost all work today is organized into bite-sized packets called projects. A project-based world is ideal for growing your brand: projects exist around deliverables, they create measurables, and they leave you with bragables. If you're not spending at least 70 percent of your time working on projects, creating projects, or organizing your (apparently mundane) tasks into projects, you are sadly living in the past. Today you have to think, breathe, act, and work in projects."[2]

Write. Perhaps the best tool to communicate your personal brand might be writing, which offers a lot of options such as features in newspapers, newsletters, and trade magazines, media that is internal to your company and external as well. The digital world provides you with the opportunity to create a blog in which you can showcase your expertise on your chosen topics. A few years ago it seemed as if everybody was rushing to start a blog, but many of these efforts fell by the wayside, making it easier to establish yourself in the blog world today. However, it takes a long time to build a readership, and you must write original content frequently—a minimum of once a month.

Speak. Are you a natural public speaker? Then you should develop these skills even further and start building a range of content you can talk about. You can also develop various formats ranging from a lunch talk to a full-day workshop. As with writing, this is an opportunity to showcase your expertise. Once you have content that others appreciate, you should seek out speaking opportunities. Besides internal opportunities, you can seek out networking groups with an interest in your topics. Industry conferences often look for new speakers, especially people from companies rather than advisors and consultants, so check their web sites for calls for speakers.

Meet. Are you good with people? Then you should develop your networking skills and communicate your personal brand through interactions with others. Become known as the person who knows a lot about your given topic, and do not shy away from opportunities to help and connect other people. You should not limit this to just attending events. There are many opportunities for hosting events in which you can control the content and get close to the invited speakers and participants. This can range from informal dinners to workshops to conferences.

A combination of these communication tools would be the best to get other people talking about you in the right way. If you do these things, you will build what Tom Peters calls "reputational power." As he states, "If you were a scholar, you'd measure it by the number of times your publications get cited by other people. If you were a consultant, you'd measure it by the number of CEOs who've got your business card in their Rolodexes."[3]

You might already have recognized that these steps can be used to brand a team as well. Then you could really complete each other by doing what you do best. As a member of a team, you should still build your own personal brand, although you need to be aware that being on a bad team can negatively affect your personal ability to move ahead.

An Exercise

Let's do a little exercise. Think of an ongoing or soon-to-be-started initiative or project in which you can also work on the communication of your personal brand. Write down a short description of the project or initiative.

_____

_____

_____

How can you use this initiative to communicate your personal brand? Which tools can you use?

_____

_____

_____

Evaluate and Evolve

I mentioned that there are two key steps in building your personal brand. Here's the second, very important, step. You also need to continuously evolve your personal brand and evaluate your efforts. Start by determining what you want to achieve, and then set metrics that will allow you to measure your development. Metrics could be the number of features you write, the number of articles that mention your name, the number of hits on Google, the number of people who seek your knowledge and so forth. Decide on only a few metrics, and try to track them for three months; then re-assess.

You should also seek feedback from others. This could be a group of trusted people and/or a coach or mentor who can observe your development. You need to make sure these people really give you honest feedback on your performance.

When you feel you are on the right track with the feedback you get from others and the metrics you have decided to follow, you should set new goals for your personal brand to ensure continuous evolvement. Remember that your future personal brand is linked to the goals you set as you define what success is for you.

Let's end with Tom Peters, who concluded his article with this statement: "It's this simple: You are a brand. You are in charge of your brand. There is no single path to success. And there is no one right way to create the brand called You. Except this: Start today. Or else." I think this still holds true.

We have already touched on networking and relationships as they intertwine with open innovation as well as personal branding. In the next chapter, I will go further into how you can use your networks and relationships to achieve your goals. Hopefully, all this focus on networking will make you share my firm understanding that networking is an important skill that can be applied to many functions and for many reasons.

Key Chapter Takeaways

- Everybody has a personal brand; taking control of your brand creates freedom and opportunities, and it is imperative for you to achieve your goals.
- Analyze the people who inspire you, in order to understand what aspects these role models have that you might want to bring to your personal brand.
- The two key steps in building your personal brand are to create the brand and then communicate it.
- To develop your personal brand statement, define your strategic goals, analyze your values and traits, solicit input on your brand from those close to you, check your digital footprints, and identify your unique contributions. From this information, you can build a brand statement that serves as your personal elevator pitch.
- It is important to know the environment in which your personal brand operates by focusing on competitors and influencers.
- Performing, writing, speaking, and meeting are key tools you should use to communicate your personal brand.

15

Strengthening Your Network

I want you to think and reflect on networks and the value they have for you in terms of enhancing your ability to be a strong leader in an open innovation environment, for communicating your personal brand, and for bringing you closer to your vision of success. Let me begin by sharing my own history and experiences with this.

Helping others connect and create value through relationships is a great passion of mine. It started in the late nineties where I met Julie Meyer, an American in London missing her network back home. This prompted her to start First Tuesday, which was a network organization aimed at helping IT-related entrepreneurs reach their business dreams. In 18 months, First Tuesday grew from a cocktail bar in London to 150,000 members on six continents. I approached Julie Meyer before it really took off. We had good chemistry and could use each other. Before long, I was the head of the Danish organization, which I helped build to seven staff members and more then 4,000 members. I also helped develop the Nordic region and stayed close to our headquarters in London. This gave me an incredible network within venture capital and entrepreneurship.

A few years later everyone was talking about nanotechnology. I quickly learned that Tim Harper was Mr. Nanotech in Europe. I invited him to Denmark to do a workshop and introduced him to relevant people here. Our relationship developed, and soon I was on board an ambitious project to create a European-wide nanotechnology network. It turned out to be too ambitious, and before long

I went back to my own projects. Nevertheless, during the time I was involved, I had built a high-level nanotechnology network, and I added new angles to my personal brand as a result of much press coverage that I got during the First Tuesday project.

Another great networker is my good friend, Kenneth P. Morse, who is a very central person in the Boston, Massachusetts, business ecosystem as managing director at the MIT Entrepreneurship Center. He is also the most extraordinary networker I have ever seen. He is just great at creating—and maintaining—relationships in ways that create value for all involved. He is an international ambassador; I introduced Ken to the Danish system, and although more activities could have developed, I am pleased to see the impact Ken and MIT have had on so many people in Denmark.

You might ask how you can connect with someone who is so much more influential than yourself. My best advice is that you play to their Rolodex, wallet, and ego. Can you help them get in touch with the local influencers in your country within the given field? Can you help them make money? Organizing a workshop or an event is a great tool for doing this, and it also allows you to get close to the influencer because you need to be in touch frequently while organizing the event. Setting up press-coverage opportunities for the influencer creates an extra boost for the ego.

The common thread that runs through all my networking experience is that I picked up issues in which I was really interested and that at the same time presented interesting business opportunities. Then I identified the key people within those areas and connected with them, making sure I had something to offer them in return. My point is that you should get involved in work that you really care for and start mapping the ecosystem and the people driving it. If you can connect with just a few key people—the influencers—within any given area:

- You have a much better chance for development on all levels.
- Your skill set will develop because you are bound to learn new things from such people.
- Your personal brand will be enhanced by being associated with the right people, and it will become even easier to connect with more of the right people.
- New opportunities will come your way, and your company will also get a lot of new opportunities, creating a win-win situation for all involved parties.

Besides creating relationships with influencers, you should also be aware of how this activity will make you look within your company. If you do this over several years, people will start to view you as someone who is well connected and influential within your chosen field and niche. You will have enhanced your personal brand.

We all have experienced how having the right relationships and the associated visibility has worked for others, sometimes to our own detriment. Have you ever asked yourself, "Why did Peter Colleague get that job rather me? I am much better qualified." Yes, you might have better skills and experience, but do you have the relationships that can put those qualities to work? And have you built relationships that make your qualities visible to the people who make the decisions in your company? Peter Colleague has this covered, giving him an edge with regard to advancement and new opportunities.

Let us look into what you should know to get this edge.

Three Types of Networking

When you plan your approach to building an effective network, it's important to realize that you actually need three different types of networks. Writing in the *Harvard Business Review*, Herminia Ibarra and Mark Hunter identified three forms of networking based on their study of 30 emerging leaders:

- Operational networking.

    Geared toward doing one's assigned tasks more efficiently. When in operational-networking mode, you will cultivate stronger relationships with individuals whose roles make them stakeholders in the work you're trying to accomplish.
- Personal networking.

    This involves engaging with people outside your organization to learn and find opportunities for personal advancement.
- Strategic networking

    This is networking that is done in the service of business goals. At this level, you create a network that will help uncover and capitalize on new opportunities for the company. The ability to move to this level of networking turns out to be a key test of leadership.[1]

    Ibarra and Hunter sum it up in the following chart.[2]

	Operational	Personal	Strategic
Purpose	Getting work done efficiently; maintaining the capacities and functions required of the group.	Enhancing personal and professional development; providing referrals to useful information and contacts.	Figuring out future priorities and challenges; getting stakeholder support for them.
Location and Temporal Orientation	Contacts are mostly internal and oriented toward current demands.	Contacts are mostly external and oriented toward current interests and future potential interests.	Contacts are internal and external and oriented toward the future.
Players and Recruitment	Key contacts are relatively nondiscretionary; they are prescribed mostly by the task and organizational structure, so it is very clear who is relevant.	Key contacts are mostly discretionary; it is not always clear who is relevant.	Key contacts follow from the strategic context and the organizational environment, but specific membership is discretionary; it is not always clear who is relevant.
Network Attributes and Key Behaviors	Depth: building strong working relationships.	Breadth: reaching out to contacts who can make referrals.	Leverage: creating inside-outside links.

Maximize Your Networking Efforts

As you work to build your operational, strategic, and personal networks, here are several tips on how to maximize the effectiveness of your networking efforts:

- Only network if you have a purpose.

    I strongly encourage you not to listen to the people who say you should network with everyone within sight so as to not risk losing any opportunities. You are already busy, and time is the most precious thing you have, so do not spend time on activities that do not serve a higher purpose.

This also goes for networking groups, which can be very useful. However, you should only join such a group if you have a purpose. It is also just fine to leave the group once that purpose is fulfilled.

- Learn to "turn on the switch"—even if you're an introvert.

Some people believe only extroverts can become good networkers. However, psychologists classify introverts as people who gain energy from being alone. It does not matter how outgoing or shy they may or may not be. This is true in my case. I would categorize myself as an introvert. I like to be by myself. I have no problem at all meeting other people, but I prefer to be by myself or with my family. My trick, and the trick introverts must use, is that I can turn on the switch and go into a networking mode. I have learned networking techniques, and I believe that having to work harder than natural extroverts has made me a better networker.

You can become a better networker by investing in a better understanding of how networking works and how you can use networks to meet your goals. Let me share a few tips on how to turn on the switch before you go to an event or a conference:

- Do your research before you go to an event. Know whom you want to meet, and be prepared.
- Everyone seeks upward connections when they're networking. If people you want to connect with see you as "inferior," they will think you are wasting their time. And networking time is often very limited. However, most people are polite and will give you one minute. So have your pitch ready and be prepared to make the most of your brief opportunity. If you are prepared, things will go much easier even for introverts.
- Do the necessary follow-up work as soon as possible.
- Leverage the power of six degrees of separation to reach anyone in the world.

This refers to the idea that if a person is one step away from each person they know and two steps away from each person who is known by one of the people they know, then everyone is an average of six steps away from each person on Earth. Think of someone who could really influence your career, and see how many steps it would take you to connect with that person.

You'll often be surprised that you don't even need six steps; it can often be done in just three or four connections.

Here's how this works in terms of networks. Networks clump people together with other people who share the same values or have a common area of expertise. The larger group usually only has a few people connecting outside this group; these people are the brokers or bridge builders who connect groups with other groups. The role of brokers explains how six degrees of separation works. If you connect with a bridge builder, that person will then connect you with another bridge builder, and so on and so on until you reach the person you want to reach. You can become very valuable by becoming a broker yourself. Also, connecting others creates friction, which creates new ways of thinking and prosperity, so for innovation leaders and intrapreneurs, being a broker can be particularly valuable and exciting.

- Use virtual tools.

A growing number of online tools and services seem to make networking so much easier. Beware; this is tricky. Many people tell me that they do see how they can get value out of virtual tools, but there seems to be a generation gap. The young working generation will use online social networks in all aspects of their work once they are allowed to do so. People aged 28 and above need to consider what kind of impact this will have in future years.

I use LinkedIn, the largest online business networking site, which is great for managing my network, although I have not found much value besides being able to reach outside my own contacts. However, the addition of features such as Q&A and Groups have made it more worthwhile spending time on LinkedIn as you get good opportunities to learn new things and share your own insights.

- Understand informal versus formal network leadership.

You need to know the influencers who are not on the formal organization chart. These are the people who hold disproportionate influence on other people. They are especially important if you are working on corporate change programs or building an innovation culture. Get to know the powers behind the throne in any formal network you join.

- Reason, ask, and tell.

    Prepare reasons for getting in touch with other people. This goes both ways. Once an interaction such as a brief encounter or a meeting is over, you should always remember to ask people how you can help them and let these people know of any ways they might be able to help you. Nothing happens if you do not ask.
- Speak-write-meet.

    Which communication "medium" will you use to build your brand and networks? Some people are great speakers, others write very well, while others are great with people. Find your strength, and build on that. Consider teaming up with others to cover all aspects. This is especially relevant if you are working in a team in which you can apply many of the ideas in the previous chapter for what we could call team branding.

Personal Network Analysis

I have come to the conclusion that the best way to help others develop networking skills is to focus on real-life cases in which I—and the other participants if it is a workshop—can help with suggestions on how to deal with networking issues. Coaching over a longer period is actually the best way of helping people develop their networking skills. In workshops, I use the personal network analysis that follows to help participants better understand their networks.

First, in the Names column write down the names of up to 20 people to whom you turn for information or for help in solving problems in connection with your job. The people do not have to have a direct connection to your work sphere.

Next, consider the kinds of knowledge and expertise (K/E) that you would have to access to in order to reach your goals. Write down the kinds of knowledge and expertise and transfer the different types to the horizontal row (K/E 1–8).

Specify which people you contact for which type of expertise. Finish off by summing up the total number of expertise types for each person (horizontally), and the total number of each expertise type (vertically).

Expertise/ Names	K/E 1	K/E 2	K/E 3	K/E 4	K/E 5	K/E 6	K/E 7	K/E 8	Total
1.									
2.									
3.									
4.									
5.									
6.									
7.									
8.									
9.									
10.									
11.									
12.									
13.									
14.									
15.									
16.									
17.									
18.									
19.									
20.									
Total									

Use of the Network: Influence and Action

Are you very dependent on a small number of people? Is your network lacking within areas that are important to you? If so, what can you do to change this?

Influence	Possible action

You now have a blueprint for leveraging the power of your existing network and for building and strengthening your network so that its power matches your goals and vision of success.

Networking in the Real World

In this interview, Lars Hinrichsen worked as a Senior Director, Innovation Projects at Chr. Hansen when he shared his views with me on networking and relationships and how this reflected on his work. Chr. Hansen is a world-leading developer of natural ingredient solutions such as cultures, enzymes, and colors. Later, Lars Hinrichsen was named the CEO of the Danish Meat Research Institute. In part, this promotion came as a result of creating a good personal brand and by networking within the Danish food industry.

What does it take to be a good networker?

Hinrichsen: I see networking very much as "give and take," and this requires that you be willing to open up. When you open up and give something in a particular situation you will also get the opportunity to let other people help you in particular situations.

Another important thing is that you must build relationships with other people. In networking, there is a strong social element, and you have to qualify for a certain level of trust. It is also important that there be a kind of common platform or what you could call the mission for the network or relationship. As a good networker you should relate to that and be able to contribute.

How do you define your network in terms of size and closeness?

Hinrichsen: It changes over time, and it is actually only in the past years that I have started to think of it as a network. You could say that my network mainly consists of three parts: A technical network, a leadership network, and a social network. Having a research background, my technical network is probably the largest and the most global one. My leadership network is much more personal and has over the years been

(continued)

built mainly with direct relations to colleagues from various job positions and business partners. The social network is family and friends.

You are on the board of the alumni organization from your MBA school. Why did you join this organization? What kind of issues are you dealing with at the alumni organization?

Hinrichsen: I was encouraged to join the board after graduation. So I started out with a very open mind and put on the working gloves ready to take my turn. Three years later, it is now obvious that the main purpose is to create a fruitful framework for networking among the alumni. This especially revolves around high-quality learning forums based on evening events with company cases and subsequent debates.

Actually, one of our issues is to find a good balance between networking and post-MBA education. We have probably been too focused on the education part and not sufficiently aware of the networking part.

Do you belong to other networking groups? If yes, which are they and what do you get out of it?

Hinrichsen: As you know, I am in one of your Danish network groups for innovation leaders. I have also recently participated in the "Innovation Roundtable," which is a Scandinavian initiative from Copenhagen Business School. I am also in a few technical networks.

INTRAP is a professional network focusing on innovation leadership, and I have learned a lot from challenges and solutions presented from other companies. I am not so active in the technical networks, which are mainly about staying updated on the food technology area in Europe.

Do you use any online networking tools? If yes, which and how?

Hinrichsen: I am on LinkedIn as is the rest of the world. I guess I am on a learning curve—or getting older—because I have not really seen the value yet. However, it is fantastic that you can read about people you know and follow their endeavors.

What are the challenges you face in using your network?

Hinrichsen: I do not regard myself as a particular good networker, but I want to learn and become even better at this skill. I have always admired people who have this talent.

What specifically makes it difficult for you to be a good networker?

Hinrichsen: I think it is very dependent on who you are as a person. I guess I can best describe my situation with the "reception syndrome." At these events I simply do not know what to do with myself, and I cannot come up with any particularly interesting things to talk about. Maybe you know the feeling. You should mingle and be introduced to new people. But how do you do that? And I think in a network you should break down the barrier and realize that the people you meet also would like to meet you, and more importantly that it is okay that you swiftly move on to the next introduction. Actually I take the opportunity to exercise these things when I go for receptions.

Can you give examples of how other people have asked for your help? Or situations in which you contributed much?

Hinrichsen: It is usually about guiding people on to other people who can help the one having a need. You can say that I often act as a mediator. In other cases, I have had the competence needed in a particular situation. This is often about giving qualified feedback to problems. The science world is very much about networking and peer reviewing, so I guess I am a part of this.

Can you give examples of how you use your network and relationships for long-term strategic purposes? This could include work as well as career development.

Hinrichsen: In my various job positions, I have always tried to build relations to peers in other companies. You learn a lot from that. Specifically, I have had good experiences working more strategically in cases where I had to navigate under changed regulatory or politically new situations.

Can you give a specific example of this?

Hinrichsen: It is difficult to get into the details. But the introduction of a new allergen legislation in the EU surely made me activate my network. In this case, it was not the lobbying aspect but more how other companies in practice deal with a new and very complicated legal situation without burdening the entire supply chain.

(continued)

On career development, I must admit that I have not been very conscientious about that with regard to my network.

What do you believe is the most common misperception about networking?

Hinrichsen: Talking about networking is very popular these days. It might be a misperception that being in the right network will make everything flow well for you. It always starts with you and what you can offer. Take a look in the mirror and ask yourself "Why would anyone invite you inside a network?"

Key Chapter Takeaways

- Accept the reality that in today's business world, networking is a critical tool for becoming the best innovation leader you can be.
- Choose networking opportunities that relate to issues that are of significant interest to you and that also present interesting business opportunities.
- Develop operational, personal, and strategic networks.
- Only network if you have a purpose.
- Realize that being an introvert need not impede your ability to be an effective networker.
- Leverage the power of six degrees of separation to add important people to your network.
- Use virtual tools to extend your networking reach.
- Perform a personal-network analysis to create a blueprint for leveraging the power of your existing network and to set goals for strengthening your network over time.

CHAPTER

16

Sell Your Vision and Ideas!

As an innovation leader, you always have something to sell. In the end it is a product or a service, but during the development of your revenue generator, you have to sell your vision to internal and external stakeholders. In this chapter, we will look at how you will communicate that vision by:

- Developing a value proposition that can be adapted for various stakeholders.
- Capturing the very essence of the value proposition in a brief elevator pitch that focuses on the recipients of the message.

Geoffrey Moore is a Silicon Valley-based consultant and author of the now-classic book *Crossing the Chasm*, which describes the issues new products or services face when they are being brought to market, and, more importantly, offers strategies on how to overcome these issues. Let's look at some of his ideas.

The Value Proposition

In *Crossing the Chasm*, Moore uses the term *value proposition* as a way to describe what we choose from among what is presented to us for consideration, including choosing nothing at all if it does not improve our current situation. The value proposition presents ways we can use our time, energy, and resources in pursuit of our goals. Our task is to evaluate whether one value proposition is better than what we are already doing or whether one is best among other value propositions available. Knowing what constitutes a value proposition guides us in our evaluation of the various alternatives.

Moore describes six elements that are needed to communicate an effective value proposition. The elements are:

1. For (target customer).
2. Who are/wants/needs (statement of needs or opportunity or compelling reason to buy).
3. The (product name) is a (product category).
4. That (statement of key benefits).
5. Unlike (primary competitive alternative).
6. Our product (statement of primary differentiation).

Moore used the high-performance computing company Silicon Graphics' early entry into Hollywood to create an example of what a value proposition might look like based on these six elements:

- For postproduction film engineers who are dissatisfied with the limitations of traditional film editors, our workstation is a digital film editor that lets you modify film images any way you choose.
- Unlike workstations from Sun, HP, or IBM, we have assembled all the interfaces needed for postproduction film editing.[1]

Moore suggests this approach because it allows you to convey all the important aspects without providing too much information. It also enables you to explain your product or service in a few sentences. The idea is that if you can convey your message to others in 60 seconds or less, they will remember the majority of the value proposition. Since word of mouth is one of the biggest forms of communication, this is extremely important. The value proposition created for this approach can also be used later when creating the elevator pitch.

Remember that a value proposition should focus on the gains you can provide your audience or customers. It is not about you and your reasons to sell something. Try also to keep it simple by focusing on a well-defined target group and its need. Also, focus on one key benefit, even though you can probably mention many, and focus on only one—or very few—competitors.

Most importantly, this statement must not be hype or something you just make up. It must be grounded in the real world. The statement has a lot of value for management purposes because it is extremely helpful in making sure we are all on the same page. Eventually, you will find that this will get hyped for sales and marketing purposes, but I suggest you keep it as clean as possible for the earlier internal purposes.

While working on your value proposition, you should try to start of with—or at least include—words such as *we help* as this will help you focus on your audience and their needs.

Now, let's do a little exercise. Think of your offerings or important messages, and ask yourself whether you are focusing on yourself or on the ones you want to influence. With your offerings or messages in mind, write the words *We help* on a sheet of paper and then try completing the sentence. Make several versions of it. Having done this, you can work further with Moore's formula.

Now you have been given a short introduction to the value proposition. I hope you sense how strong a tool this can be and why it is important for innovation leaders and intrapreneurs to understand.

The Elevator Pitch

You start with a vision that helps you understand why you are doing what you do. The value proposition then helps everyone talk from the same page. Now you are ready for the elevator pitch.

An elevator pitch (or elevator speech) is an overview of an idea for a product, service, or project. The name reflects the fact that an elevator pitch can be delivered in the time span of an elevator ride. When I do exercises, we work with 60 seconds, because I find 30-second pitches too superficial to be useful.

The term *elevator pitch* is typically used in the context of an entrepreneur pitching an idea to a venture capitalist. Venture capitalists often judge the quality of an idea and team on the quality of its elevator pitch, and they will ask entrepreneurs for the elevator pitch to quickly weed out bad ideas

You should use an elevator pitch to get your foot in the door with key stakeholders who can influence your offering or message. This is important. An elevator pitch is not about making a sale; it is about getting a chance to explain your offering or message in further detail at a future meeting. Do not try to sell now, and do not get into details. Just get a meeting.

You have many types of stakeholders, such as partners, customers, and colleagues, so you should make versions of your pitch for each of kind of stakeholder—or even better for each individual you target.

I often tell teams I work with that they should set up a war room in which they put up posters of their key targets and write down all the information—business as well as personal—they can get on them. This could include information such as:

- Why are they relevant for your offering?
- How might they specifically help you if they like your offering?
- What are their business facts (company facts, position within in the company, organizational structure, and contact information)?
- Whom do they know?
- Whom do you know that can get you in touch with the target or someone within that circle?
- Where can you run into the target (conferences, cafés or restaurants, transportation)?
- What is their public profile (Google, articles, speeches)?
- What are their personal interests?
- Do you or someone on your team have something in common with the target?
- Does the target have a history of helping other people in the way you wish them to help you?
- Can you get in touch with people they've helped before and ask them about their experience with the target? What worked for them?

This should of course also be stored online, but it helps to be able to visualize your key stakeholders in the war room or in your office. Okay, not many teams do the visualization part, but you should definitely do the information exercise. The more you know about your target, the better you can prepare for the potentially once-in-the-lifespan-of-your-project opportunity to make the impression that gets you to the next stage that might make all the difference for what you do.

You will most likely never get to use an elevator pitch in the true sense, because you will almost always have more than a minute to make your case when you interact with others. Then you might think that there is no need to do this. Wrong. The key purpose of value propositions and elevator pitches is their preparation. The learning you gain while defining your value proposition and tuning your pitch will make you understand your product, service, or message so well that it will become much easier for you to achieve success. That creates all the reasons in the world to take this very seriously.

Picture this: You have worked on an idea that can really make a difference at your company. Nevertheless, you keep hitting the wall of corporate indecisiveness. After having given yet another so-so presentation to people who seem unable to make a decision, you step into the elevator with the person who can single-handedly decide whether you idea is boom or bust. You know this is your big—and perhaps only—shot. Your pulse quickens. Your body temperature rises. What do you do?

Too few people are prepared to deal with such a situation. They have not given it much thought, let alone prepared something to say or rehearsed saying it. So instead of capitalizing on the opportunity, they just let it walk out the door or they mess it up and end up looking like incompetent fools. Do not leave this to luck. Prepare. Prepare. Prepare.

What should you include in a pitch? This is my shot:

- Introduce yourself properly.

  Introduce yourself in a proper manner and get a confirmation that the person is who you think he or she is. Beware of your body language. During role-play exercises at workshops, I am amazed how many people do not really pay any attention to that.
- Find a hook.

  You should find a hook or an angle that is personal and gets the person intrigued to listen to you even though he or she is busy. It could be that your target has given a speech or written an article that you have heard or read. Make a reference to that. This opens up the conversation and at the same time plays to the target's ego. Not all people have such high profiles, but your research should give you some nugget of information that enables you to start with something that shows you have taken the time to get to know this person. Do not exaggerate, because some people might find this intrusive.

- Explain the big picture.

Frame the big picture in a plain and simple way that does not get into details or technical talk. An example: "We specialize in providing utility cost-saving solutions for top-tier companies in the beverage and dairy industries. Our offerings help companies reduce utility costs by 10 to 20 percent, which not only improves bottom lines on an average of 3 to 4 percent, but also reduces CO_2 emissions."

- Make it specific.

Follow up on the big picture by focusing on the pain or the opportunity for the target. Remember this is not about your compelling reason to sell, but the compelling reasons why the target should listen further to you.

An example: "We took the time to get to know your company a little bit, and we understand you have annual utility costs of about $19 million. Would you say this is correct?"*(You need to be sure this is correct. Wait for some kind of acknowledgement from the target before you move on).* "Okay. Then we believe that you can save $2.2 million over three years. This is a 2.8 percent improvement of your bottom line. Would you like to know more about this?"

Of course he or she would like to know more, giving you another yes answer. Try to ask questions that your target can answer positively. This keeps the target in a more positive state of mind.

Now you have quantified the big picture in specific terms for the target, and you are ready to close the conversation.

- State how you do it, why you are different, and close the conversation.

Give a brief explanation of what you do and why this is better than the current offerings or solutions on the market. The target should have an idea of such offerings, enabling you to make a positioning statement about the competition.

Now you need to close the conversation. An example: "I understand you are busy, and I will not take more of your time. May I suggest that we set up a meeting within the coming weeks? Great. Here is my card. Can I have yours? Thanks.

I will get in touch with you about a meeting as soon as I am back in the office."

Or it could be slightly different if your target is a referral person rather than the decision maker: "I understand you are busy, and I will not take more of your time. I understand the proper person to discuss this with is Cynthia Jackson, who is in charge of utility costs. Is this correct? Great. Can you help me get introduced to her? Fine. Here is my card. Can I have yours? Thanks. I will get in touch with her about setting up a meeting with Cynthia and other relevant persons as soon as I am back in the office."

- Follow-up.

Remember to follow up quickly and competently. You might need to be quite persistent here, as busy people do not always reply on the first e-mail or phone call. There might also be another reason than just busyness. If your target gets many solicitations, he or she might not respond until you have proven that you are persistent and dedicated. It can take several attempts of trying to get in touch to prove your persistence.

Key Chapter Takeaways

- Becoming skilled at formulating value propositions and elevator pitches is an invaluable tool for innovation leaders and intrapreneurs.
- A good value proposition is grounded in reality, not hype, and provides all the important aspects of your offering without providing too much information.
- An elevator pitch is an overview of an idea for a product, service, or project that can be presented in roughly 60 seconds.
- Always do your homework on the stakeholders you need to reach so you have relevant information for a conversation when you meet them.
- When meeting a stakeholder, introduce yourself properly, explain the big picture, make it specific to the stakeholder, and then state how your offering works and how it is different from other offerings.
- Know how to appropriately close the conversation, and make sure you follow up promptly on the promised action.

17

Corporate Business Plan Competitions

Corporate business plan competitions are primarily designed to help companies identify and nurture the skills of intrapreneurs. But they can also help build and refine skills that will support open innovation. Such competitions help people learn to innovate across an organization, eliminating silos and fostering relationship-building capabilities. Skills built in running internal competitions can then be used to leverage the power of external competitions as part of an open innovation effort. This bonus chapter explains how to implement such a competition in your organization.

Corporate business plan competitions are patterned after the business plan competitions run by educational institutions such as MIT and Harvard Business School. But the idea can be adapted for a corporate environment or even used to drive open innovation. Companies that have successfully used this strategy to foster intrapreneurship include Danfoss Ventures, Novozymes, and computer giant Hewlett-Packard. Such programs can:

- Increase revenues and raises profits, both short and long term.

    Intrapreneurs are at their best when they are challenged with new ventures or projects. Business plan competitions can make this link and when combined with solid execution strategies can produce revenues and profits.

- Support recruiting efforts.

  A committed focus on intrapreneurship as evidenced by a business plan competition improves the corporate image and makes it easier to attract and retain top talent.

- Encourage others throughout the company to focus on innovation.

  Visibly identifying and cultivating intrapreneurs through a business plan competition can shift the corporate culture so that everyone stays alert and always searches for opportunities that might otherwise be lost.

How It Began

Danfoss's business plan contest is called the Man on the Moon competition. It was designed to identify and develop intrapreneurs as well as new business ideas. It all started when, in 2004, I was having ongoing conversations with Hanne Arildsen, who was in charge of Danfoss Ventures. Her challenge was to move from looking for great business ideas outside the company to capitalizing on valuable ideas generated by Danfoss employees. Hanne liked my idea of creating an internal business plan competition that would pull together teams of employees who would develop and present business ideas that the executive management team would judge.

I thought it was important to include a great story to inspire people in a corporate setting. My inspiration was John F. Kennedy and how he had proposed landing a man on the moon within a specific time period. One part of his speech to the U.S. Congress on this topic seemed a particularly apt metaphor for the Danfoss Ventures situation:

> I believe we possess all the resources and talents necessary. But the facts of the matter are that we have never made the national decisions or marshalled the national resources required for such leadership. We have never specified long-range goals on an urgent time schedule, or managed our resources and our time so as to insure their fulfillment.[1]

Getting the first competition off the ground at Danfoss was not easy, particularly because we were determined to go from idea to execution in just two months. Many people questioned whether the company actually had enough people who fit the description of good intrapreneurs. Others said we should take more time and do more planning, but we believed things could happen faster and wanted to show that it was possible to make a difference in a short time.

Today, the Man on the Moon competition has become an annual event. It has been highly successful in identifying over 20 active ideas with a combined multibillion-dollar potential. Furthermore, the competition has been vital in identifying potential intrapreneurs at Danfoss. The company has matched this newly discovered talent with idea pools that have emerged from the competitions to create a good prospect for success.

Hewlett-Packard Jumps In

Inspired by the Danfoss model, the Imaging and Printing Group of Hewlett-Packard launched its own business plan competition in 2006. It is called Flashpoint, and, according to Bill Wagner, who headed the program, it was designed to:

- Spread entrepreneurial spirit throughout HP's worldwide employee base.
- Teach business planning skills to HP's tech-savvy inventors.
- Identify and recognize entrepreneurial individuals.
- Generate high-quality business proposals.
- Facilitate a cultural message that Effective Innovation = Technology Innovation + Solid Business Skills

Wagner said that when he first started pitching Flashpoint 2006, it wasn't an easy sell. "Nothing like this had been done before at HP, and it took me a while to become effective at selling the value proposition," he said. "Everyone is very busy, so a new cultural initiative like this can be viewed as a distraction. But in time I got the support I needed, and it ended up being very successful. Getting support for Flashpoint 2.0 was easy. We have a track record now, and our management is solidly behind the idea."

Novozymes initiated a business plan competition named "Intrapreneur Cup: Dream-Dare-Do" in 2007. The program was aimed at developing new game-changing ideas as well as the skills of potential intrapreneurs. The competition drew strong interest from all parts of Novozymes with teams from four continents as well as all business units.

Building Your Competition

Although each company's business plan competition is uniquely its own, these 10 steps are necessary for any successful competition:

Step 1: Form a steering committee.

This group will be responsible for planning and implementing the competition. It will also be responsible for setting the competition's future—and strategic—direction. The steering committee should have people who are enthusiastic about the idea and who are well connected to key people and executives. It is also best if they are willing to roll up their sleeves for intensive work during the planning and execution stages. Committees with five to seven people work well.

Step 2: Establish goals for the initiative.

Know what you hope to accomplish. This will help you manage the expectations of company leadership and competition participants. You also must clearly define what you expect from the participants, not just during the competition, but afterwards as well.

For example, at Danfoss Ventures, we expected people to start working full-time on the ideas that were identified in the competition. But some of the participants were vice presidents and already had heavy responsibilities; they weren't interested in personally moving their ideas forward. Clarifying these expectations before you start is important.

Step 3: Define the size of the competition.

It might be best to start off with a relatively small program and plan to grow in size in subsequent years. Starting with a small pilot will enable you to get the initiative off the ground faster. Also, it will make it easier to make quick adjustments as you proceed.

The size of the competition also impacts how well you're able to manage expectations. How many business ideas might you be able to move forward? What happens if you get five great ideas but only have the resources to move two of them forward?

Considering this in advance will guide you in determining how big the competition should be.

Step 4: Define what's in it for participants, including winners and also-rans.

How will you reward people for participating in business plan competitions? How will this help them advance in your company? Will you offer monetary awards to the competition winners? You need clearly defined benefits for all participants and for the winning team. Participating in a business plan competition is time consuming and stressful. People need to know what they stand to gain from participating.

The companies I have been involved with have given rewards such as a cash award of a month's salary or a weekend trip for the participants and their spouses. However, the most important rewards are those that help drive a career forward. This begins with overall recognition through internal and external communication channels. It should also include the opportunity to join a network or program for intrapreneurs, and, most important, the participants should be given the chance to work on new business ideas.

You should lay out the nontangible benefits that come with participating in this learning experience. These might include any competencies for which you'll be providing training during the competition, such as teamwork, innovation processes, presentation skills, and management of high-risk projects. Highlighting the professional-skill-building aspect should help support your recruiting efforts.

Step 5: Identify a theme that will motivate and inspire people to participate.

Because each corporate culture is different, only you know what type of inspirational message will speak to employees at your company. Build a communications strategy in advance that leverages this theme and informs people about why the competition is good for the company and for participants.

For the first competition at Danfoss, the CEO set the challenge that the participants should think of business ideas for Danfoss should the price of oil reach more than $100. Often you get better results when you put some kind of restraint on your innovation efforts.

Step 6: Establish a competition schedule.

As you schedule the steps of the competition, consider any timing issues related to your particular company. To the extent possible, you will want to avoid times of the year when key events are happening, which will make it difficult for people from across the organization to participate.

The major milestones on your schedule should include the following:

- Announce competition and open recruitment phase.
- Provide deadline for applicants.
- Announce chosen participants.
- Announce competition kickoff.
- Midterm—announce selection of finalists who will present to the jury.
- Final—present the finalists to the jury and selection of winner(s).

In general, a competition should last about four months from kickoff to the final event. This will give participants time to make serious progress while keeping the intensity.

Step 7: Establish the recruitment process.

What types of people do you want to recruit? What process will you use to get people to apply? How will you choose the group you invite to participate from among all applicants? These key questions must be answered before you start publicizing the competition.

In the competitions I've been involved with, the recruiting process included a written application followed by interviews conducted by members of the competition's steering committee and external contributors. Identifying potential intrapreneurs is not a simple task. It requires having a well-trained interviewing team whose members understand what you're looking for and how to ask questions that elicit the right information about applicants. Remember that, at this stage, you're looking for people, not ideas.

In both the written application and in interviews, generic questions in corporate speak will not do the job. Questions should get people to describe specific examples about how they, as individuals, have achieved something, been agenda setters, and worked with passion and drive.

An important consideration is whether you'll have people apply as individuals or as teams. I strongly advise against recruiting teams, because companies that do so usually end up having to make a lot of compromises. For example, if a team of three applies and during the process you identify that one member of the group doesn't have the X factor you're looking for, what do you do then? Do you compromise your standards and take in the team to gain the two people who do have the X factor? Or what if a team comes to you with an idea already in mind and you think it's actually a pretty good idea, but you don't think the team members are quite up to the standards you've set for the competition? Again, you're in an awkward position, and if you end up making too many compromises, your whole initiative will be in trouble.

On the other hand, if you recruit individuals with strong intrapreneurship traits and then form them into teams (or let them form themselves into teams), these people will generally find an idea that fits your competition, and you won't have to make any compromises in your recruiting.

Finally, have in place a Plan B, just in case recruiting does not go as well as you hoped it would. This may involve identifying people in advance who you would like to have in the competition and making personal phone calls to them to encourage them to apply if they don't do so on their own. If you have to go this route, you'll need to have your messages ready to answer their concerns about the competition.

For example, some people don't apply simply because they got distracted from completing the application. A simple phone call can get them back on track. Others may be worried about the time commitment the competition will require. Still others may wonder if they're the type you're looking for. For both these groups, be ready to answer their concerns. It's important to make it clear that you're not looking for right-stuff managers but rather for people who are different or who have certain characteristics that will make them good intrapreneurs.

Step 8: Set evaluation criteria for judging the proposals developed by the competition teams.

In addition to defining the judging criteria, you'll also have to determine what evaluation method you will use. For example, Novozymes found much inspiration in the MTOR-model, which looks into factors such as market potential, technology feasibility, resource needs, and organizational fit. Overall impression was added as the last—and most important—criteria. Each criterion is rated and weighted based on its importance. Questions are developed for each criterion to ensure that jury members are all defining the criterion in the same manner.

The criteria should be different for the midterm event, which is used to make sure the participants are serious and are making progress. The teams that do not do so should be eliminated at this stage. Besides progress, you should also look at presentation skills at the midterm, because you do not want to bring a team that is not able to communicate well to the final judges, who should be company executives.

Step 9: Assemble the judging panels.

Here is a perfect spot for furthering the overall objective of your innovation effort by showing that your business plan competition has the support of people in the highest tier of company leadership. Tap the highest-ranking people you can to serve as your competition jury. Having the rare opportunity to expose their talents to senior executives will go a long way toward assuring that your recruiting effort draws the best and the brightest in your company.

If you follow the model of having a midterm where you select the teams that will go forward to the final, you'll want one judging panel for the midterm and a different one for the final. At Novozymes, they use the steering committee and a few external consultants to do the midterm judging. Then the final is judged by a panel of senior executives, including the CEO.

Step 10: Put coaches in place.

The final piece you need to put in place before you're ready to kick off your business plan competition is a set of experts who can coach the teams during the competition. You'll want to make two types of coaches available:
• Team coaches.
   These people have knowledge that is relevant for the ideas pursued by the teams. They are first assigned when

the teams have decided on their idea and have had it approved by the steering committee, if required. The steering committee should assign coaches to the teams based on their understanding of the teams, the ideas, and the competences within company. Team coaches should be internal people, so that they will have an overview of other ongoing company activities related to the idea. Coaches should be prepared to spend at least 10 to 15 hours with their teams during the course of the competition.

- Competency coaches.

  These people are skilled in specific areas such as taking new products or services to market, stakeholder management and networking, developing a value proposition, or financial issues. The teams should be able to choose competency coaches as they see fit. However, recommendations should be given by the steering committee based on what they've learned about the teams during the selection phases. In some competitions, teams are given a budget to spend as they wish on competence coaches or on market research or on other information that would help them.

Create a Vehicle for Open Innovation

Finally, another important next step to consider for future competitions is the involvement of external partners. The competitions have been highly successful as internal initiatives, but imagine what you could create if you were able to form open innovation teams consisting of your own employees and external people from customers and partners.

If your company is the driver of such an activity, you have an innovation engine that could be very effective in not only listening to the needs of the external ecosystem of customers and partners but also turning this input into business ideas and stronger relationships with key partners. Yes, intellectual property rights will be an important issue in such scenarios, but being in control of the competition will make it easier to model and manage this process according to your interests. The logistics of bringing in outside people may at first seem daunting, but in many cases the companies that have undertaken business-plan competitions are already global in scope and have successfully dealt with many of the issues that managing an around-the-world project requires.

Whether you have undertaken an internal business plan competition or one that involves external entities, you are certain to reap the rewards of new and profitable innovations and a better-trained group of intrapreneurs who can help you foster even more innovation in years to come.

Implementation

Once you have undertaken all these steps, you are now ready to put your business plan competition into motion. There are three key milestones of the execution phase, the kickoff, the midterm, and the final.

Kickoff Event

Your business plan competition officially gets under way with an event that brings the selected teams together for a session that will tell them what to expect from the competition and what you expect from them. Another key goal of this event is to generate excitement and enthusiasm among the competitors as well as throughout the organization via publicity about the kickoff. These events usually include a day and a half to two days of activities. You will, of course, make liberal use of your competition theme in the kickoff, using it as a communications platform for the activities you organize.

Every organization has its own take on how to organize the kickoff, but most include these elements:

- Orientation for the teams regarding the details of how the competition will work, what resources will be available to them, and what the company expects of them in the months ahead.
- Introduction of the team and competency coaches.
- Team building exercises to help the teams coalesce.
- Work on building a common language among participants around innovation and other key topics such as the elements of the business plans they will create.
- Training in skills that will be important for success in the competition.

- Involvement by senior executives to reinforce the importance of the competition and the company's strong interest in it.

The team-building exercises should challenge the mindset of the participants and give them a taste of what is to come in terms of having to cope with uncertainties and with running into unexpected roadblocks. For example, at Danfoss we included a team building exercise in which teams worked on a problem at their own tables for a period of time and then traded tables and worked on the problem solution that another team had started. Now, they suddenly had to deal with an unexpected situation like those that routinely arise in the real world of innovation.

You want teams to form together fast. Some team members might know each other already, but perhaps not well enough to face the stress of working closely together over the next few months. Working together as a team during the kickoff will help begin to build the strong bonds that are necessary for a team to hold together when the going gets rough.

Spending time on building a common language is extremely important. This will help ensure that the participants are all on the same page as the steering committee regarding the mission of the competition and the outcomes the company desires. At Novozymes' kickoff, for example, a consultant who has been working with the company on a model called MTOR (market, technology, organization, and resources) made a presentation to competition participants that helped them understand the need to consider these key elements in their work together.

The skills training portion of the kickoff event should be the start of a learning program that carries through the entire competition. You will have identified the different skills that participants will need to master at the different stages of the competition when you selected the competency coaches. Consider having each coach make a presentation at the kickoff. Sample skills to focus on could include crafting a value proposition and an elevator pitch, using internal and external relationships, and making a presentation.

Once you get into your second competition and beyond, consider including a session in the kickoff in which former participants can provide tips and advice to the new participants. You might also have last year's winning team give the presentation they made in the final to model what will be expected of this year's participants.

As a preparation to the kickoff event, the steering committee should also evaluate the initial business ideas from the teams. This discussion includes considering the ideas from the corporate point of view and bringing relevant information to the table to which the teams might not be privy. For example, the committee might review ideas as to how they match with something else going on in the organization. They also might consider whether the idea is something that's been tried multiple times before and never worked. Also, the capabilities of the team should be part of the equation. A question to consider is "Can a team deliver on what it's promising?"

Based on this discussion, a team might be told to go back to the drawing board for a new idea. For example, one team at Novozymes was asked to find another idea because the market for their original idea was fairly small and a lot of work had already been done in the target industry without much progress. Obviously, these considerations should be worked on before the kickoff event.

Midterm

After the kickoff, the teams begin working together to develop their business ideas. To help ensure they're doing the necessary hard work and staying on track, you'll want to stage a midterm evaluation in which teams face the risk of being eliminated. This event is also a chance to provide more learning opportunities for the teams through sessions with the various coaches.

Frequently a two-day event, the midterm might feature a rehearsal of team idea presentations on the first day and actual presentations on the second day. The jury you've selected will evaluate the presentations, and then may decide to eliminate some teams at this stage. The chief focus at this point should be on how well the team is able to answer the question, "Why is this a compelling idea?" At this stage of the game, they should be able to respond quickly and effectively. Usually, you have four or five teams in the competition. This should be cut to three teams after the midterm to keep some competitiveness and provide more quality for the executives in the final jury.

Again, you'll want to generate internal publicity about the event to keep the whole organization aware of the competition. This might be a good point to work with your corporate communications staff on stories on the individual teams. Such stories can go a long way to encourage other employees to enter the competition in future years.

One possibility to consider in terms of helping build excitement about the competition is to have open presentations at the midterm and the final, at which you have an audience of interested employees. This idea may not work at a company that has different levels of confidentiality, but, where possible, it should be considered. Allowing the general audience members to ask questions of the team members can be quite interesting. At the midterm, in particular, such questioning may help the teams improve the content of their presentations or even further refine their ideas.

Final

After the midterm, the teams will continue to work on their ideas and their presentations of those ideas until the final. Presentations to the executive judging committee at the final are usually 20 minutes long. The judges then usually take an hour or more to discuss ideas and vote on them.

Once a winner is selected, it's time to celebrate their success, both at the final and in internal and even external publicity. In fact, all the teams should be honored for the hard work they put into the competition. This public recognition can play a key role in motivating others to participate in your next competition and can even be a strong recruiting tool. For example, Danfoss Ventures is located very remotely in Denmark, and recruiting is always a challenge. They have used their competition in full-page recruiting ads to communicate how innovative they are and the fact that they are a company where you'll have an opportunity to take chances and grow.

Postcompetition Decisions

The choices you make after your business plan competition are very important. Your key short-term and long-term decisions include:

- How will the ideas from the competition, particularly the winning idea, be moved forward?
- What role will the competition teams have from this point on? Will they have the opportunity to continue to work together to

make their idea a reality, or can they be involved with other innovation projects?

- How will you capitalize on the relationships and camaraderie that developed during the competition? Will you form a talent pool or internal network that will be offered networking and learning opportunities? Should this be opened up to qualified applicants, including those who were not admitted to the competition itself?

If you go through the process and have a jury of top executives who are committed to the results, you should come out of the competition with a platform on which the idea can be turned into a reality.

The choice of whether the competition team moves the idea forward or whether it is turned over to someone else is specific to the company involved. Some companies have chosen to use the teams from the competition as a talent pool whose members can be matched with good ideas generated anywhere in the company. They act as intrapreneurs in residence, awaiting a project that is appropriate for them to lead while continuing with their current jobs.

Key Chapter Takeaways

- Corporate business plan competitions can help increase revenues and raise profits, support recruiting efforts, encourage an organization-wide focus on innovation, and prepare an organization to undertake external competitions.
- The key steps involved in starting a competition are:
  - Form a steering committee.
  - Establish goals.
  - Define the competition size and what participants will gain from competing.
  - Establish a schedule and a recruitment process.
  - Identify an inspiring theme.
  - Establish judging criteria and choosing the judges.
  - Identify team and competency coaches.
- Introduce your competition with an exciting kickoff event.
- Use a midterm event to narrow down the selection of ideas.

- Make sure senior executives are involved in judging at the competition final.
- Make important postcompetition decisions, including:
  - How will the ideas from the competition, particularly the winning idea, be moved forward?
  - What role will the competition teams have from this point on?
  - How will you capitalize on the relationships and camaraderie that developed during the competition?

18

The Review

EVERYTHING IN ONE EASY PLACE

I've put the takeaways from all the chapters in one place to make it simple for you to periodically review how you're doing in terms of moving forward on your path to being the best innovation leader or intrapreneur you can possibly be. Good luck on your journey and please don't hesitate to contact me at Stefan@intrap.com if you have comments or questions about the topics I've written about in this book. I would welcome the chance to exchange ideas and opinions with you about the challenges you face as an innovation leader or intrapreneur.

Chapter 1: Why Open Innovation Matters

- The 24/7 global economy and the increasing transparency of knowledge are driving the movement toward open innovation.
- Internal and external resources need to work hand-in-hand to make open innovation happen.
- Open innovation should be a hot topic in every company because the idea of combining internal and external resources to increase innovation productivity and prowess is just too good a value proposition to miss out on.
- There are champs, contenders, and pretenders in the open innovation world, with as many as 60 percent of companies falling in the pretender category.

- To move out of the pretender category and into the contender category, you must do these things:
  - Ask why your company should be involved in open innovation. Open innovation works only if your reasons align with the overall corporate strategy.
  - Define what open innovation is.
  - Remember your people. A paradigm shift like this requires that employees change their mindset and obtain new skills.

Chapter 2: What Open Innovation Looks Like

- The form open innovation takes varies dramatically from company to company.
- Open innovation is about bridging internal and external resources throughout the entire innovation process to make innovation happen.
- The real differentiator in the various forms of open innovation is the level of involvement from external partners, customers, or suppliers.
- Open innovation is about integrating external partners in the entire innovation process.
- User-driven innovation is highly related to open innovation, but it has to go further in bringing external partners to the whole innovation process to become open innovation.
- User-driven innovation and open innovation can be a powerful combination.
- The chief benefits of open innovation are:
  - Speed the development of new products and services and thus increase revenues and market share.
  - Shorten time to market for new products and services and accelerate profits.
  - Reduce direct spending on R&D.
  - Improve the success rate of new products and services.[2]
- Three fundamental questions must be answered before embarking on a journey toward open innovation:
  1. What will open innovation do to your business model?
  2. How will your organizational chart change to accommodate open innovation?
  3. What does this mean to your role as manager or leader?
- Trust is fundamental to open innovation.

- The need to build trust as a basis for successful open innovation means that it is more relevant to look at the people side of innovation than to concentrate on processes, and it also brings more power to the people who really drive innovation within a company.

Chapter 3: How to Approach Open Innovation

- Your answer to the question of why your company should try open innovation needs to address how open innovation can be an important part of the general innovation strategy, which in turn needs to be highly aligned with the overall corporate strategy.
- The paradigm shift entailed with open innovation requires that people change their mindset and obtain new skills.
- Innovation should be about more than just core products and services, and it should involve as many business functions as possible rather than just R&D and sales and marketing.
- The elements of open innovation include:
  - People who can manage relationships with customers and partners.
  - Willingness to accept that not all the smart people work in your department or even for your company, and a corresponding willingness to find and work with smart people both inside and outside the company.
  - Willingness to help employees build the knowledge and understanding of how an idea or technology becomes a profitable business, perhaps by developing a job-rotation program that could even engage partners and customers.
  - Understanding that failures represent opportunities to learn, and a willingness to reward those efforts and that way of learning.
  - Dismissing NIH (not invented here).
  - Willingness to strive for balance between internal and external R&D.
  - Willingness to be a risk taker rather than being risk averse, while using common sense to balance the risk level.
  - Accepting that open innovation does raise intellectual property issues. Your legal team can choose to play either offense or defense.

- Understanding that open innovation requires open communication. Work around the confidentiality and intellectual property rights issues to create an environment built on trust.
- Not needing to always be first. Building a better business model is better than getting to market first.
- Open innovation not only requires a different mindset; it also requires new skills that include:
  - Holistic point of view—the X-vision.
  - Networking.
  - Making an effective elevator pitch.
  - Managing stakeholders.

Chapter 4: First Things First

- You only get one-and-a-half chances to do open innovation right, so you must prepare carefully.
- The key elements that must be put in place before moving forward with an open innovation initiative include:
  - A clear mandate, a strong strategic purpose, and an ideation theme.
  - A stakeholder analysis.
  - A communication strategy.
  - A shared language about innovation in your company.
  - Organizational approaches that achieve TBX (top down, bottom up, and across).
  - Adopt an attitude of striving to *be* innovative vs. working to *become* innovative.
- Your open innovation mandate should:
  - Lay out the resources and authority given to the innovation team.
  - Clarify how potential conflicts are to be handled.
  - Encourage stakeholders to solve problems, such as resource allocation and commitment, without involving executives.
- Make sure your strategic purpose answers this key employee question, "What's in it for me?"
- Establish a scope or theme for idea generation that will prompt ideas in areas that match the organization's innovation goals.
- Bring in the O (outside) factor in addition to TBX.

- Build your company's innovation DNA with real initiatives that convince all stakeholders that their contributions are valued.
- Help employees believe that your company is innovative by sharing great stories.

Chapter 5: How to Identify and Develop the People Who Drive Open Innovation

- When it comes to making innovation of all types happen, people matter more than ideas.
- Companies need two different types of people for innovation initiatives:
  1. Innovation leaders who work on the strategic and tactical level to build the internal platform required to develop organizational innovation capabilities.
  2. Intrapreneurs who work on the operational level to turn ideas and research into real products and services that move the business forward.
- When identifying people who will be outstanding innovation leaders and intrapreneurs, look for optimists who have passion and drive, and who are curious and believe in change. Also look for people who have a talent for networking, strong communication skills, and an ability to deal with uncertainty. For innovation leaders, also look for people who see the big picture.
- To find such people, ask prospects questions that will reveal:
  - How up to date they are on their professional field.
  - How they've overcome obstacles to make things happen.
  - Whether they are open or defensive and combative.
  - How customer-oriented their thinking is.
  - If they are capable of building on their basic skills so their perspective of innovation will be broadly based.

Chapter 6: The Networked Open Innovation Culture

- A networking culture is a critical part of an innovation culture that aspires to become more and more open and external-oriented. Your company needs to have strategies in place to build networking expertise within your organization.
- Even if you're not using an open innovation model, employees who are operating in a global community need to know how to network with people in far-flung locations.
- A networking culture has:

- A clear statement of strategic reasons people need to develop and nurture internal and external relationships.
- Leadership commitment to networking.
- Networking initiatives that mesh closely with your corporate culture.
- Frequent virtual and face-to-face opportunities for people to polish their personal networking skills.
- Pay close attention to the three types of networkers in your organization: central connectors, brokers, and peripheral people.
- Deploy Web 2.0 applications to facilitate networking internally and externally.
- To maximize the effectiveness of face-to-face networking:
  - Emphasize short length, high frequency.
  - Turn sessions into idea platforms.
  - Help managers keep their eye on the big picture so they don't cause roadblocks because they worry that their employees who are networking are taking time away from their "real work."
  - Make quick decisions on ideas contributed to idea marketplaces.
  - Use wiki-style project sites to blend the real and the virtual.
- Avoid these roadblocks to building a networking culture:
  - Not enough time or skills.
  - Lack of focus, commitment, structure, and communication.
  - Bad gatekeepers.
  - Insularity.

Part II: Roadblocks

Chapter 7: Why Top Executives Do Not Get Open Innovation— and What to Do about It

- Senior executives are often major roadblocks to innovation because they:
  - Are focused on short-term gains.
  - Missed out on innovation education.
  - Are risk averse
  - Are control freaks.
  - Lack the X-vision.
  - Don't understand why a networking culture is important.

- Are too far away from the action when it comes to innovation.
- You can overcome these problems by:
  - Challenging and stretching the mindset of top executives.
  - Helping them understand and buy into the creation of a tight link between innovation strategy and the overall corporate strategy.
  - Understanding what really matters to top executives.
  - Leveraging the power of corporate communications.
  - Gaining some small wins and not starting too many innovation initiatives at once.

Chapter 8: Defeating the Corporate Antibodies

- Because change frightens many people, the prospect of change caused by innovation often causes the eruption of corporate antibodies.
- Corporate antibodies are most likely to arise during the incubation and acceleration phases of innovation.
- You can fight corporate antibodies by:
  - Making people backers rather than blockers.
  - Staying below the radar.
  - Having frameworks and processes in place.
  - Providing high autonomy to your innovation councils.
- Stakeholder management is a key component of fighting off corporate antibodies. You should:
  - Identify and profile all stakeholders.
  - Communicate with your stakeholders.

Chapter 9: Radical Innovation as a Roadblock

- Companies that are in the early stages of establishing their innovation capabilities may be biting off more than they can chew if they pursue radical innovation because:
  - It can take too long to produce results.
  - In most organizations, few people on any level have successful experiences with radical innovation.
  - Projects that are somewhere in the range between incremental and radical innovation are more acceptable to risk-adverse executives and managers.
  - It's easier to achieve radical innovation by buying a start-up and integrating it into your company.

- Market-leading companies prefer to play it safe rather than cannibalizing and reinventing themselves.
- To pursue radical innovation successfully, companies must:
  - Have a corporate strategy with room for radical innovation and adequate time to implement that strategy.
  - Have people who can execute on radical innovation projects and processes in place to make them happen.

Part III: Personal Leadership for Open Innovation

Chapter 10: Defining Success

- To fulfill your role as innovation leader to the greatest degree possible, you must define success, know how to make change happen, identify your values, manage relationships and time, and communicate your messages.
- The key pathways to your success include:
  - Following your passion.
  - Setting your personal vision and then identifying the goals that help you achieve it.
  - Identifying the people who will help you achieve your vision, and building mutually beneficial relationships with them.
  - Working on your T-shape, and keeping abreast of external developments that affect your personal vision and goals.
  - Building and communicating your personal brand and messages.
  - Managing your time.

Chapter 11: Know Your Values

- Your ability to achieve success is linked to having a clearly defined set of values that drive the choices you make in your work and personal life.
- Taking time to reflect upon and define your values is an invaluable exercise.
- It is important that your values and those of the organization in which you work be aligned. Otherwise, you will be forced into the uncomfortable position of role playing at work with little chance of achieving your career goals.
- Living each day in a way that is consistent with your values clears your path to success.

Chapter 12: Making Change Happen

- Your ability to change the trajectory of your career depends on two factors:
  1. The balance between how you view yourself and how others view you.
  2. The relationships you have built.
- If there is a perception imbalance, you can change it by:
  - Realizing and acknowledging your issues and committing to change.
  - Understanding the difference between push and pull when it comes to change.
  - Setting goals and prioritizing them.
  - Building accountability into your change effort—and beginning to change others' perceptions of you—by communicating your goals to key stakeholders.
  - Creating rituals to enforce change.

Chapter 13: Managing Time

- Take time periodically to reflect on how you're budgeting your time; make sure you're allocating this precious resource in ways that maximize your chances of achieving success.
- Control your time; don't let others control it for you.
- Keep Parkinson's Law in mind, and make sure you're not stretching tasks out longer than actually necessary. When delegating work to others, realize that they, too, will usually take the full amount of time you allot to complete a task, so set deadlines that are realistic but tight.
- Use the 80/20 Rule to evaluate where you get the most value from the time you spend. Make note of activities that are not pushing you toward success, and outsource or even eliminate them.
- Leverage the power of solitary reflection; set aside at least one hour each week to think deeply about a specific issue.

Chapter 14: Polishing Your Personal Brand

- Everybody has a personal brand; taking control of your brand creates freedom and opportunities, and is imperative for you to achieve your goals.

- Analyze the people who inspire you in order to understand what aspects these role models have that you might want to bring to your personal brand.
- The two key steps in building your personal brand are to create the brand and then communicate it.
- To develop your personal brand statement, define your strategic goals, analyze your values and traits, solicit input on your brand from those close to you, check your digital footprints, and identify your unique contributions. From this information, you can build a brand statement that serves as your personal elevator pitch.
- It is important to know the environment in which your personal brand operates by focusing on competitors and influencers.
- Performing, writing, speaking, and meeting are key tools you should use to communicate your personal brand.

Chapter 15: Strengthening Your Network

- Accept the reality that in today's business world, networking is a critical tool for becoming the best innovation leader you can be.
- Choose networking opportunities that relate to issues that are of significant interest to you and that also present interesting business opportunities.
- Develop operational, personal, and strategic networks.
- Only network if you have a purpose.
- Realize that being an introvert need not impede your ability to be an effective networker.
- Leverage the power of six degrees of separation to add important people to your network.
- Use virtual tools to extend your networking reach.
- Perform a personal-network analysis to create a blueprint for leveraging the power of your existing network and to set goals for strengthening your network over time.

Chapter 16: Sell Your Ideas and Vision!

- Becoming skilled at formulating value propositions and elevator pitches is an invaluable tool for innovation leaders and intrapreneurs.

- A good value proposition is grounded in reality, not hype, and provides all the important aspects of your offering without providing too much information.
- An elevator pitch is an overview of an idea for a product, service, or project that can be presented in roughly 60 seconds.
- Always do your homework on the stakeholders you need to reach so you have relevant information for a conversation when you meet them.
- When meeting a stakeholder, introduce yourself properly, explain the big picture, make it specific to the stakeholder, and then state how your offering works and how it is different from other offerings.
- Know how to appropriately close the conversation, and make sure you follow up promptly on the promised action.

Chapter 17: Corporate Business Plan Competitions

- Corporate business plan competitions can help increase revenues and raise profits, support recruiting efforts, encourage an organization-wide focus on innovation, and prepare an organization to undertake external competitions.
- The key steps involved in starting a competition are:
  - Form a steering committee.
  - Establish goals.
  - Define the competition size and what participants will gain from competing.
  - Establish a schedule and a recruitment process.
  - Identify an inspiring theme.
  - Establish judging criteria and choosing the judges.
  - Identify team and competency coaches.
- Introduce your competition with an exciting kick-off event.
- Use a midterm event to narrow down the selection of ideas.
- Make sure senior executives are involved in judging at the competition final.
- Important postcompetition decisions include:
  - How will the ideas from the competition, particularly the winning idea, be moved forward?
  - What role will the competition teams have from this point on?
  - How will you capitalize on the relationships and camaraderie that developed during the competition?

Appendix A

THE TEN TYPES OF INNOVATION™

Innovation Category	Innovation Type	Description of type	Business example
Finance	1. Business model	How you make money	Dell revolutionized the personal-computer business model by collecting money before the consumer's PC was even assembled and shipped (resulting in net positive working capital of seven to eight days).
	2. Networks and alliances	How you join forces with other companies for mutual benefit	Consumer-goods company, Sara Lee, realized that its core competencies were in consumer insight, brand management, marketing, and distribution. Thus it divested itself of a majority of its manufacturing operations and formed alliances with manufacturing and supply-chain partners.
Process	3. Enabling process	How you support the company's core processes and workers	Starbucks can deliver its profitable store/coffee experience to customers because it offers better-than-market compensation and employment benefits to its store workers, who are usually part-time, educated, professional, and responsive people.

Innovation Category	Innovation Type	Description of type	Business example
	4. Core processes	How you create and add value to your offerings	Wal-Mart continues to grow profitably through core process innovations, such as real-time inventory management systems, aggressive volume/pricing/delivery contracts with merchandise providers, and systems, which give store managers the ability to identify changing buyer behaviors and to respond quickly with new pricing and merchandising configurations.
Offerings	5. Product performance	How you design your core offerings	The VW Beetle (in both its original and its newest form) took the market by storm, combining multiple dimensions of product performance.
	6. Product system	How you link and/or provide a platform for multiple products	Microsoft Office bundles a variety of specific products (Word, Excel, PowerPoint, etc.) into a system designed to deliver productivity in the workplace.
	7. Service	How you provide value to customers and consumers beyond and around your products	An international flight on any airlines will get you to your intended designation. A flight on Singapore Airlines, however, nearly makes you forget that you are flying at all, with the most attentive, respectful, and pampering preflight, inflight and postflight services you can imagine.
Delivery	8. Channel	How you get your offerings to market	Legal problems aside, Martha Stewart has developed such a deep understanding of her customers that she knows just where to be (stores, TV shows, magazines, online, etc.) to drive huge sales volumes from a relatively small set of home-living educational and product offerings.

9. Brand	How you communicate your offerings	Absolut conquered the vodka category on the strength of a brilliant "theme and variations" advertising concept, strong bottle and packaging design, and a whiff of Nordic authenticity.
10. Customer experience	How your customers feel when they interact with your company and its offerings	Harley-Davidson has created a worldwide community of millions of customers, many of whom would describe being a Harley-Davidson owner as a part of how they fundamentally see, think, and feel about themselves.

Appendix B

OPEN INNOVATION EXAMPLES
AND RESOURCES

This is a list of examples and resources that I find useful in my work with open innovation. I hope you find this useful. Let me know if you believe something is missing.

Corporate web sites – examples of open innovation and crowdsourcing-like initiatives:

3M Zukunft Innovation (in German)
> www.zukunft-innovation.com

BMW Virtual Innovation Agency
> www.bmwgroup.com/via/

Campbell's Ideas for Innovation
> www.campbellsoupcompany.com/ideas/

Cisco I-Prize
> www.cisco.com/web/solutions/iprize/index.html

Clorox Connects
> clorox.hivelive.com/pages/home

Colgate-Palmolive
> www.colgate.com/app/Colgate/US/Corp/Innovation.srv

Dell IdeaStorm
> www.ideastorm.com

DSM Licensing
> www.dsm.com/en_US/html/dlc/home_dlc.htm

Ericsson Labs
> https://labs.ericsson.com

General Mills G-WIN
  openinnovation.generalmills.com

GlaxoSmithKline
  innovation.gsk.com/gsk/ctx/noauth/PortalHome.do

Hershey's Ideaworks
  www.hersheys.com/contactus/ideas/

HP Labs Open Innovation Office
  www.hpl.hp.com/open_innovation/

IBM Collaboration Jam
  www.collaborationjam.com

Huawei
  www.huawei.com/partners/seeking_partners.do

Intuit Collaboratory
  www.intuitcollaboratory.com

Intuit Labs
  intuitlabs.com

Johnson Controls Open Innovation
  www.johnsoncontrols.com/publish/us/en/products/
  automotive_experience/open_innovation.html

Kraft – InnovateWithKraft
  brands.kraftfoods.com/innovatewithkraft/region.aspx

LG
  www.lgtce.net/33+M52087573ab0.html

Medtronic
  www.medtronic.com/innovation/idea-submission/
  index.html

Nestlé
  www.nestle.com/NestleResearch/GlobalRnD/OpenInnovation
  AndPartners/OpenInnovationAndPartners.htm

Netflix Prize
  www.netflixprize.com

Nokia
  research.nokia.com/openinnovation

P&G Connect+Develop
www.pgconnectdevelop.com

Pepsi Refresh Project
www.refresheverything.com

Philips
live.philips.com

SAP
www.sdn.sap.com/irj/scn

SAP – Sapiens (In German)
www.sapiens.info/

Sara Lee
www.openinnovationsaralee.com/Pages/Home.aspx

Shell GameChanger
www.shell.com/home/content/innovation/bright_ideas/
game_changer/

Siemens
www.siemens.com/innovation/en/about_fande/cooperations
.htm

Starbucks – MyStarbucksIdea
mystarbucksidea.force.com/home/home.jsp

Unilever
www.unilever.com/innovation/collaborating/

Weyerhaeuser
www.growingideas.com/#/innovation/

Open innovation intermediaries and platforms:

Big Idea Group
www.bigideagroup.net/

Chaordix
www.chaordix.com

EdisonNation
www.edisonnation.com

Exnovate
www.exnovate.org/

Hypios
www.hypios.com

Ideas4All
www.ideas4all.com

IdeaConnection
www.ideaconnection.com

IdeaWicket
www.ideawicket.com

InnoCentive
www.innocentive.com

InnoGet
www.innoget.com

MillionBrains
www.millionbrains.com

NineSigma
www.ninesigma.com

Pharmalicensing
pharmalicensing.com

TekScout
www.tekscout.com

Topcoder
www.topcoder.com

Yet2.com
www.yet2.com

Your Encore
www.yourencore.com

Open innovation software:

Fellowforce
www.fellowforce.com

Imaginatik
www.imaginatik.com

Spigit
  www.spigit.com

InventionMachine
  www.inventionmachine.com

Inno 360
  inno-360.com

Open innovation conferences:

Open Innovation Conference by Marcus Evans
  www.marcusevans.com/html/eventdetail.asp?EventID=
  16381&ad=openinnov2010&SectorID=19

CoDev–Co-Development and Open Innovation
  events.roundtable.com/codev/

Open Innovation Summit
  www.worldrg.com/showConference.cfm?confCode=MW10004

Media, resources and tools:

Alltop
  alltop.com

Blogging Innovation by Braden Kelley
  www.business-strategy-innovation.com/innovation-blog.html

BusinessWeek
  www.businessweek.com

Financial Times
  www.ft.com/home/europe

Harvard Business Review
  hbr.org/

InnovationTools by Chuck Frey
  www.innovationtools.com

LinkedIn
  www.linkedin.com

MITSloan Management Review
  sloanreview.mit.edu/

TweetDeck
  www.tweetdeck.com

Notes

Chapter 1: Why Open Innovation Matters

1. Larry Huston and Nabil Sakkab, "Connect and Develop: Inside Procter & Gamble's New Model for Innovation,"*Harvard Business Review* 84 no. 3 (March 2006).

Chapter 2: What Open Innovation Looks Like

1. Joachim Ebert, Sumit Chandra, and Andreas Liedtke, *Innovation Management: Strategies for Success and Leadership* (Chicago: A.T Kearney, 2008),1.
2. Ibid.

Chapter 4: First Things First

1. http://net.grundfos.com/doc/webnet/challenge/downloads/8714_ Assignment.pdf (July 2009).
2. 2005 Toyota Annual Report, 26 (http://www2.toyota.co.jp/en/tech/its/vision/).

Chapter 5: How to Identify and Develop the People Who Drive Open Innovation

1. O'Connor, Gina Colarelli O'Connor, "Research Report: Sustaining Breakthrough Innovation," *Research-Technology Management,* 52, no 3(2009): 12–14.
2. Rob Cross, Robert J. Thomas, and David A. Light, "Research Report: High Performer Networks—How Top Talent Uses networks and Where Rising Stars Get Trapped." http://www.robcross.org/pdf/roundtable/high_performer_ networks_and_traps.pdf.
3. Marc Andreesen, "How to Hire the Best People You've Ever Worked With." http://blog.pmarca.com/2007/06/how_to_hire_the.html.

Chapter 6: The Networked Innovation Culture

1. Sarah Millstein, "Now, Brevity Is the Soul of Office Interaction,"*New York Times,* November 21, 2008.
2. Rob Cross, Andrew Hargadon, Salvatore Parise, and Robert J. Thomas, "Together We Innovate,"*Wall Street Journal,* September 15, 2007.

3. Michiae Chui, Andy Miller, and Roger Roberts, "Six Ways to Make Web 2.0 Work,"*McKinsey Quarterly*, February 2009.
4. Stan Schroeder, "Facebook Users Are Getting Older. Much Older." July 7, 2009, http://mashable.com/2009/07/07/facebook-users-older.
5. Cross et al., "Together We Innovate."

Chapter 7: Why Top Executives Do Not Get Innovation, Much Less Open Innovation— and What to Do About It

1. Corey Criswell and Andre Martin, "10 Trends: A Study in Senior Executives' Views on the Future," Center for Creative Leadership, 2007, 6.
2. Criswell and Martin, "10 Trends," 7.
3. "CEO Turnover Remains High at World's Largest Companies, Booz Allen Study Finds," Booz Allen press release, May 22, 2007, http://www.boozallen.com/news/3608085.

Chapter 10: Defining Success

1. http://www.artsjournal.com/artfulmanager/main/008344.php.

Chapter 11: Know Your Values

1. http://humanresources.about.com/od/success/qt/values_s7.htm.
2. Ibid.

Chapter 12: Making Change Happen

1. http://www.slowleadership.org/blog/2008/07/the-dangers-of-setting-yourself-goals/.
2. Tal Ben-Shahar, *Happier:Learn the Secrets to Daily Joy and Lasting Fulfillment* (New York: McGraw Hill, 2007), 9.
3. Ben-Shahar, *Happier*, 10.

Chapter 14: Polishing Your Personal Brand

1. http://www.fastcompany.com/magazine/10/brandyou.html?page=0%2C1.
2. Ibid.
3. Ibid.

Chapter 15: Strengthening Your Network

1. Herminia Ibarra, Mark Hunter and "How Leaders Create and Use Networks,"*Harvard Business Review*, January 1, 2007.
2. Reprinted with permission from Harvard Business Publishing. From "How Leaders Create and Use Networks" by Herminia Ibarra and Mark Hunter.

Harvard Business Review, November 2007. © 2007 Harvard Business
Publishing; all rights reserved.

Chapter 16: Sell Your Vision and Ideas!

1. Geoffrey Moore, *Crossing the Chasm,* (Mankato, MN: Capstone, 1999), 150.

Chapter 17: Corporate Business Plan Competitions

1. John F. Kennedy, Special Address to Congress on the Importance of Space,
   May 25, 196

About the Author

Stefan Lindegaard is a speaker, network facilitator and strategic advisor who focus on the topics of open innovation, intrapreneurship, and how to identify and develop the people who drive innovation.

He runs several network groups for people working on the intersection of leadership and innovation, including leaders from global companies such as Bang & Olufsen, Lego, and Novozymes. He is also the founder and facilitator of 15inno Group on LinkedIn, which counts more than 800 global corporate innovation leaders.

Stefan Lindegaard believes open innovation requires a global perspective, and he has given talks and worked with companies on open innovation in Europe, the United States, and Asia. His blog is a globally recognized destination on open innovation. You can read further at www.15inno.com.

Index